SECRETS
FOR TRAVEL
SURVIVAL

SECRETS
FOR TRAVEL
SURVIVAL

OVERCOMING
THE OBSTACLES TO
ACHIEVING PRACTICAL
TRAVEL FUN

EUGENE R. EHMANN

New York

Secrets for Travel Survival

Overcoming The Obstacles to Achieve Practical Travel Fun

ISBN 978-1-60037-465-4

Library of Congress Control Number: 2008929707

MORGAN · JAMES
THE ENTREPRENEURIAL PUBLISHER

Morgan James Publishing, LLC
1225 Franklin Ave., STE 325
Garden City, NY 11530-1693
Toll Free 800-485-4943
www.MorganJamesPublishing.com

In an effort to support local communities, raise awareness and funds, Morgan James Publishing donates one percent of all book sales for the life of each book to Habitat for Humanity. Get involved today, visit www.HelpHabitatForHumanity.org.

Table of Contents

Preface

Travel. The word conjures up images for us all. It can mean something as simple as traveling to the store, or it can mean going on vacation or going around the world.

This travel thing isn't as simple as it sounds. Of course, I'm just having some fun with that. But it *is* true that we use the word a lot of different ways.

The word "travel" is a verb, noun, or adjective. As a verb, it is both transitive and intransitive. These are some of the meanings:

1. to go from one place to another, as by car, train, plane, or ship; take a trip; journey: *to travel for pleasure*
2. to move or go from one place or point to another
3. to proceed or advance in any way
4. to go from place to place as a representative of a business firm

And there are seven other uses!

It's the summer of 2009, and there is *so* much going on around the world. There seem to be so many more natural disasters: cyclones, earthquakes, hurricanes, tornadoes, flooding. We're hearing accounts of tens of thousands of people perishing from these all over the world. Tragedy abounds in China, Burma/Myanmar, Mexico, Peru, and the Midwestern United States.

The loss of human life and liberty is rampant in Darfur, several other African nations, (Did you know there was a Congress of Oppressed Nations back in 1918?) Kashmir, and Myanmar. There is still strong political division within many nations that, for some in those countries, equates to oppression, lack of freedom. In the name of "keeping the peace," crowd control is still resulting in the deaths of thousands. Civil unrest doesn't even begin to describe what is happening.

For the United States, September 11, 2001, brought about untold, irreversible change. For the entire world, the petroleum crisis has been significant. Recognize that the United States is just beginning to experience high fuel costs while of the rest of the western world has been living with confiscatory fuel prices for years.

Now U.S. airlines are reorganizing. Some have gone bankrupt and reorganized. Some airlines are combining. Because of rising fuel costs, for the first time, some airlines are charging for checked baggage. Flight service is changing: some cities are being eliminated from service, while most airlines are reducing the number of flights to most cities.

Sound melancholy, especially when even thinking about pleasure travel? Well, since time immemorial, travel has continued to be part of the human expression of living. Through war, tragedy, and famine, we have continued to travel, sometimes *because* of those unhappy events. Remember, travel is for more than just

2

pleasure, though that is my emphasis. I understand the challenges, changes, and difficulties. There will always be something new in the world of travel. That's a given. But I will stand with Solomon, who said, "There is nothing new under the sun."

I'm addressing what is going on in travel right now, but these circumstances and facts change. No matter. That's right ... no matter! There are certain things I recommend and certain things I encourage. I will give tips to make much of your travel easier, less mysterious. However, the overwhelming factor for each of us in traveling—the factor that remains constant, never changing over the centuries—is *attitude*. I know, that's a much-used word and concept. Hmmm, maybe it's an important one! I love this saying: "Worry works! Nothing I've ever worried about has come to pass!" Paying attention, being alert, and studying don't have to equate to "worry." Fretting is evil, a de-energizer, and counterproductive, period! So when I say attitude, what I mean is a good attitude, an open but not empty mind, and the overall understanding that life is good, people are good (some of their actions notwithstanding), and the centerpiece of life is relationships. Travel—cross-cultural exchange—enhances living and life. That's what I mean by attitude.

Remember what may seem obvious: when we travel, we are the foreigners or strangers. Think about that! Most Americans aren't used to thinking that they are *ever* foreigners; the *other* person is. The world is centered on the United States—perhaps in Ames, Iowa, if that's where you're from. Not only do I travel going around the corner or going to the store, as an investigator, I also travel to foreign countries. And once there, I investigate cases or help conduct a raid on the bad guys. In each instance, I am literally on foreign territory. Clearly, traveling in South America is more foreign than going to the local grocery store. But isn't that in large based on our familiarity with the environment to which we travel?

What's the point? The point is that going to the store or to Grandma's is familiar, not intimidating. *Familiarity* is the big factor for us. In writing this, I want to make you more comfortable by filling in gaps in your knowledge.

I want to make travel a more user-friendly experience, more familiar. I certainly don't want to suggest that we in some way reduce the excitement of a trip to Europe, to think of it as casually as a trip to the store. My goal is to reduce the real and imagined obstacles to travel so that more of the pure excitement and joy can be experienced. For most of us, the thought of going someplace is usually a pretty welcome thought. Often, however, the actual planning takes the luster off and may even result in canceling the trip.

Let's talk through some of those obstacles and remove some of the negative mystery, and you will come out at the end of this read with a more excited or more informed view.

Introduction:
Why Should You Read My Book?

Murder, maiming, smuggling, counterfeiting. I've seen it. On the side of the law, I've been a part of it, in a very real sense. There's a verse in the bible I like in which God says, "I have set before you life and death, blessing and cursing: therefore choose life …" (Deuteronomy 30:19). I have chosen life and blessing. For me, part of life and blessing has been travel, and in this book I'm sharing part of that joy.

The opening vignette of the first chapter characterizes many of my journeys, and I'll share more of those to illustrate some of the points I'll make, but first let me tell you a little about my background.

I'm not a travel agent. I have nothing to do with the travel business. I'm just a traveler. I've traveled extensively, under a variety of conditions, using many, many different modes and over several different continents. I know about travel. I know how to make travel more—much more—enjoyable. And by reading and using this book, you'll be able to share some of the accumulated wisdom I've garnered over the years.

When I was a child, my Southern California family took frequent vacation trips by automobile, traveling into adjacent states. When I was fifteen, we made our first trip to Hawaii, flying on an airline called the Flying Tigers. Until just before we made our trip, this airline had been a freight airline composed of pilots from the world-famous Flying Tigers air unit (http://www.flyingtigersvideo.com/) and had the best safety record in the airline industry at that time, never having had a crash. That fact was very important to my father, who organized this trip.

We traveled on one of their Super Constellations, and although it was one of the fastest airliners at the time, the flight from Los Angeles to Honolulu was over eight hours, a distance of about 2,500 miles. Today, most people only see propeller airplanes on short commuter hops.

That eight hours was nothing compared to our next trip, which was to Europe, where we spent eight weeks visiting eight different countries. That jaunt, again aboard a Super Constellation, took thirty-six hours from Los Angeles to Shannon Airport in Ireland, with stops in Washington DC, Labrador, and Newfoundland to accommodate some needed engine maintenance. But more about that later.

I became a policeman at age twenty-one. I graduated first in the academy. While still in training—and then after graduating—I was assigned to the Vice Division, working undercover on gambling, liquor-violation, and sex-predator cases. I went from there to the Patrol Division, to a special patrol unit in the troubled inner city. After that, I went to the Juvenile Division … perhaps the most difficult and discouraging assignment as a policeman. Then I was recruited into the FBI, and I became a special agent.

As a policeman, I had become a firearms instructor. And as a former full-time policeman, I was something of an anomaly in the FBI. It was unusual for a new FBI agent to go right to work in "meaty" criminal matters, but such was my assignment. I began working fugitive matters and interstate auto theft.

I was then sent to a world-renowned language school located in Monterey, California—the U.S. Department of Defense's Defense Language Institute, West Coast, where I learned Spanish, again graduating first in the program. Besides a copy of *Don Quixote* in Spanish, my reward was a limited choice of assignment, and so I chose the Phoenix Division. There, I continued to work criminal cases. Surprisingly, there were few cases involving my use of Spanish.

I attended several specialized schools, where I was again certified as a firearms and defense tactics instructor, and I was sent to the first undercover school ever offered by the FBI. At that point in its history, the FBI did no undercover work. Back in Phoenix, I transferred to the Tucson Resident Agency, part of the Phoenix Division, and I then moved into working organized crime; however, with my strange combination of training, I was still called upon to go after fugitives and was involved with an occasional Spanish-speaking case.

Joseph Bonanno

After six years with the FBI, I went to work for a newly formed state agency in Arizona that was concentrating its efforts on working against organized crime and the a multi-state, federally funded agency, but I continued working very closely with several of my former FBI agent friends. After a successful three-year-long investigation of Joseph Bonanno, one of the original five Mafia family leaders (considered to have been "the Godfather"), I began traveling extensively, not only among the multiple states that comprised our agency but also to also Washington DC. There, I testified for budgets for our agency, and in front of investigative committees such as the Senate Judiciary Committee.

After five years, I left that state agency and was immediately contacted by the local ABC television affiliate to make a documentary special regarding the Bonanno investigation. For several months, we worked on that special, traveling to several cities on the East Coast of the United States and to Montreal, Canada. We ended up producing a one-hour television special, which won the Arizona Associated Press documentary of the year award.

From there I started my own consulting business, and since then, I've traveled not only to Canada and Mexico but also to Europe several times, and to most of the Latin American countries. I've consulted with major corporations and wealthy individuals, and the work included major thefts and the investigation of counterfeit products, especially those made in China and being shipped to Latin America.

My business hasn't been travel, yet I've traveled extensively because my business has *included* travel. I've had great fun doing so, and I've learned much. Most of you won't ever travel as much as I have, but wouldn't it be nice to take a trip and when you've returned home, feel quite satisfied with the experience?

When I first started traveling, I'd invariably return home and say, "I wish I'd …" or "If I go again, next time I'll …" No trip is ever perfect. There's always something that could be better. I want *your* trip to be a truly *fond* memory. If that means "productive," then so be it.

In any event, read along, and travel along with me. I promise this journey will enhance your future travel.

Chapter One
Why I Can Give You Advice

"You've got to help me !!" This was a real call from a frantic mother, and it was the nightmare of every parent. Her voice trembled, and she could just barely get the words out. "My son is a boat captain sailing in Mexican waters. He's been arrested for murder and is in prison in Veracruz. He was arrested just a few days ago. I just learned about

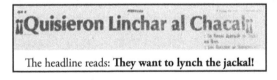

The headline reads: **They want to lynch the jackal!**

it. The newspapers are calling him a jackal, and he's going to be sentenced within the next thirty days. I think he may be being tortured. I don't know if he has an attorney, and I don't know what to do. I need you to get down there right away and see if you can help."

My partner had called me early one morning. He was the head of a law enforcement agency in one of the southeastern states.

This woman had contacted the attorney general of one of the southeastern states, who in turn had contacted my partner. I was friends with the chief federal prosecutor of Mexico, and with a number of the heads of state police agencies there. I spoke Spanish, and by that time, I had traveled extensively in Mexico and knew my way around. The rule of life there was simple and clear: don't ever get arrested in Mexico!

The laws of Mexico are based on the Napoleonic code, which is quite different from U.S. constitutional law ... way, way different, especially as applied by Mexico. As far as the American is concerned, procedures are quite different and can seem very arbitrary. Time was of the essence. I knew that in such a situation, it was imperative to get to work within the first twenty-four hours of an arrest. Here, thirty days had already passed.

It was January, and we hastily made our arrangements through a travel agency, agreeing to meet in Dallas and then travel together to Mexico City, and from there to Veracruz. What happened next is part of the reason that I decided to write something about travel.

When we got to Mexico City, we found out that our travel agent hadn't worked out the details for our connecting flight to Veracruz and had not actually confirmed our passage, or so we were told. We found out that if we wanted to make it to Veracruz within the next day, we'd have to take a bus!

That ride, taken a number of years ago, is still vivid in my memory. Now it's a fond one. It was a lengthy delay in a rather urgent journey. It's only about two hundred miles from Mexico City to Veracruz—by air, maybe an hour. By bus? It's over the Sierra Madre mountain range, passing through multiple villages along the way: a six- to eight-hour drive ... depending.

I don't know how old the bus was, but it was at the very least beat, if not "mechanically challenged." We were the only *norteamericanos* among the ten-too-many passengers, but out of politeness and humility, we were offered seats ... a treasured provision! In fact, the passengers were extremely gracious and of good humor. Based on their demeanors, I had to imagine that many made this trip regularly.

Along the way, we picked up and dropped off passengers with chickens and goats. We got to see rural Mexican life in all of its delightful rawness. We drove into the evening, and even in mild Mexican winter weather, it soon grew quite cold. Our jackets were packed and under the bus. Our shivering was noticeable, and fairly soon, the kind Mexican passengers offered us several newspapers, which we saw they were using to cover themselves as they made that cold nighttime journey in an unheated bus. There we sat on a packed Mexican bus, covered with newspapers, bouncing along through the Sierra Madre mountains, making our way east to the coastal city of Veracruz ... listening to soft clucking of caged chickens.

We met with the accused in the Vera Cruz prison...*not* a place to which you want to travel! Now, I mention all of this for several reasons. The first is to describe the extent and variety of my travel. You'll also find that it has included a mixture of contacts with business and government entities and criminals, with a sprinkling of personal touring thrown in.

Because there has been a lot of quasi-police work in my travels, I've had contact with, and even made personal friends with, customs personnel, heads of foreign police agencies, street police officers, attorneys general of several countries, directors of federal customs agencies, corporate leaders, and—the most important—local citizens.

Through my contact with each of them, I've learned a great deal about the ins and outs of travel. I've experienced wrong bookings and wrong flights, been searched and pulled out of line and searched again, and had every item of my luggage taken out; on the other hand, I've also been escorted through the entire customs and immigration processes, and I've been simply waved through searches ... but I've never lost any luggage!

I've stayed in some of the finest luxury hotels, slept in cots in facilities with no plumbing at all, and eaten in the finest restaurants and also from pushcarts on the sides of rural neighborhood roads. Under normal circumstances, no sane person would ever consider such carts as providing food fit for human consumption.

I've not suffered from any travel-related disease; I've not had adverse effects from eating local food, and in months of travel and living in (for instance) Mexico, I've never had the famous "Montezuma's revenge" (affectionately known as *Entamoeba histolytica*). As a general rule, I don't take preventative travel vaccinations, though there are clear exceptions; I've not found it necessary to take any for the last ten years of travel. I've never been lost for more than a few minutes, I've rarely been disoriented, and I have always garnered great bonus memories from my unexpected meanderings.

Fear should *not* be a component of traveling, either in the preparation or in the actual going. With the application of some common sense, some wisdom, and good preparation, you'll be able to have the pleasure of seeing, learning about, and relating to other peoples and their cultures. You'll be able to conduct business more effectively.

Let's walk through some planning and travel together.

Chapter Two
What's the State of the World?

The world, put on its ear: 9/11/2001.

I don't think I'm being either dramatic or ethnocentric when I say that the whole world changed with the events of 9/11. Yes, United States citizens tend to be ethnocentric, meaning "the belief that one's own culture is superior to all others and is the standard by which all other cultures should be measured." Yes, we believe that everything good begins in the United States and is developed and refined in the United States. We are woefully uneducated about much of anything outside of our borders. We stoutly refuse to learn other nations' languages. We *expect* everyone to speak English ... and to speak it effectively. We demand that "the mountain come to Mohammed."

That said, we *are* the world's biggest consumers. Sadly, in the eyes of much—if not all—of the rest of the world, that is our biggest plus. We consume. We also do produce a lot. We also are probably the most creative and innovative nation, in an overall general sense, in the world (though we clearly do *not* monopolize in those areas); and we do set the trends in many areas. However much debt we may have as a nation, and however much of that is consumer debt, is up for grabs. The fact is that for many years, the United States has been one of the most stable economies on Earth. I suppose some people also respond to the fact that the United States easily has the largest, best-equipped, and strongest fighting forces of all nations. Whether or not we are a "bully" nation is another subject.

I traveled to Buenos Aires in June 2001, before 9/11. Our client was a multibillion-dollar corporation and maintained a large distribution center in that city. Armed robbers invaded their fenced and guarded facility in order to steal two semitrailers of valuable goods. Our interactions there were really very cross-societal. We met with the executives of the corporation, local and federal police officers, Argentine customs officials, and eventually with the attorney general of Argentina.

Our investigation took us into Paraguay. Because of that, and because of the value of the merchandise stolen, we spent several months investigating. We eventually determined that there were elements of organized crime (yes, there is a presence of the Sicilian Mafia in Buenos Aires). And, not unlike organized crime in the United States, the criminal influence extended into the upper echelons of both private enterprise and government. That's the reason that our contacts there were so broad, and it is part of the reason that I learned a lot about their government and society.

Unbeknownst to the world and much of Argentina, their economy was on the brink of dramatic change. In June 2001, the Argentine peso was valued at roughly the equivalent of the U.S. dollar. By January 2002, that ratio began to drop dramatically, eventually arriving at a ratio of almost four Argentine pesos to one U.S. dollar.

It would be misleading to associate that economic decline in Argentina with the 9/11 attacks. However, that event resulted in very interesting comments and commentary to us, as U.S. citizens working in Argentina. Less than three weeks after 9/11 occurred, I was back in Buenos Aires. To a person, everyone expressed deep sorrow and condolences over the event. That surprised me. I was surprised because first of all, everyone spoke to the situation, and second, because they were so kind toward us about it.

Historically, from a government-to-government standpoint, relationships between the United States and Argentina were on again, off again. Within a period of three or four decades, Argentina had experienced extreme changes in government, from the fascist to communist-sympathizing leaders and dictators. The Argentine government had been sympathetic to a variety of enemies of the United States over the years. Argentina had openly supported and had economic relationships with terrorist groups, and with countries associated with al-Qaeda.

On the other hand, Argentina had also suffered at the hands of international terrorists, the two most notable attacks occurring in Buenos Aires in 1992 and 1994. Those attacks were against the Israelis and were carried out by Hezbollah groups. Nevertheless, during that same period of time a few (not all) government officials conducted official Argentine business with the same individual attackers. That kind of foreign-policy schizophrenia made it difficult for the United States.

It would be very, very easy to hear of the kind of information I've just mentioned and, as a traveler, become unnecessarily concerned or even decide to cancel one's plans. As I mentioned, to a person, everyone in Argentina responded to us very kindly regarding the losses sustained from 9/11. I'm not talking about just the merchants or the people who would stand to gain financially from befriending American travelers, but more importantly, I engaged individuals on the street, citizens next to whom I was having a cup of that wonderful Argentine espresso or of their native maté (mah-tay) tea. Some almost came to tears when they spoke of the 9/11 attacks. Point? Simply be aware that we see ourselves one way, through our filters. Consider how others see us.

Now that over six years have passed, is there doubt in anybody's mind that the whole world has adjusted to the aftereffects of 9/11? Tragic as 9/11 was, it was obviously not the first terrorist attack, right? But it was the first major terrorist attack on the United States! With that, everything changed. Security and attitudes changed as a direct result of the reactions of the United States, and they changed throughout the world. Like it or not, that's the way things have gone in this world for perhaps the last seventy-five years. As the U.S. goes, so goes the world ... to a large extent.

The World Situation

While I fully believe that there has been an increase of tragic events around the world, it's very important for us to remember (especially we Americans) that the media—and by that I mean the tremendously improved communications that we now experience—has brought to our attention skirmishes and wars and deaths and plagues that fifty years ago, we wouldn't have heard about until we read a history book.

If you couple our greater awareness of events around the world with the fact that most of the man-made tragedies have not occurred on our soil here in the United States, we find that most of us have been pretty clueless as to what plagues, war, or terrorist attacks mean to us as a nation. Virtually all other countries in the world, even the Western European countries, have had instances of foreign attacks and foreign terrorism on their soil.

All in all, the United States has lived a very sheltered and extremely abundant life. Have you ever considered that for most of its life, the United States has pretty much been an island? We have oceans on the East and West Coasts, and the north and south borders are extensive, mostly rural, and very sparsely populated. Up until perhaps fifty years ago, the flow between Canada and the United States and Mexico and the United States was gentle and friendly, for the most part. We are a nation made of immigrants, and—again, for the most part—the citizens of the world were substantially law-abiding. There was no actual need for a fence, and philosophically there was every reason not to have one.

The several wars that we've been in have not been on U.S. soil. Perhaps with the exception of the great influenza outbreak in the early twentieth century, our experience of epidemics has been all but nil. If we dare to speak or think comparatively, our poverty has been and continues to be pretty mild.

What I'm saying here may seem obvious, and it may be easy to set aside or disregard. I'm saying that considering or even meditating on these few paragraphs can be a very important step toward creating a newer and clearer filter for the way we view the people we visit on our travels.

You're Going to Travel, Eh?

Okay, so you've either found out or you've decided that you're going to take a trip. Let's assume you have a week or more to plan. The first thing that I do is to catch up on the social and political climate of the country or state to which I'm going to travel. Today, I'm a New Yorker. It would be good for me to learn a bit about West Virginia, were I to go there, and what's going on. If you really enjoy traveling, it's a good idea—and kind of fun—to know those things anyway.

We live in a small world today, don't we? Many times the events of another country can affect us in one way or another. So it's good, as a matter of general education, to know what's happening in other places in the world.

Let's consider a couple of things. First, and perhaps foremost, as a general rule, no matter what you read, *foreign countries want American dollars* and contact with Americans. Perhaps a kinder comment is that overwhelmingly, *foreign citizens are eager to receive and learn from Americans.* Yes, there are a few places where Americans aren't very well-liked. But even there, the citizens of those countries are inundated with American products, American media, and American habits. As a result, their curiosity and interest in things American mostly overrides any animosity they may have toward us. Add to that the fact that in many nations, tourism is the country's biggest source of income. But "America" is different from an individual American.

Second, there are many, many ready sources of information about the different nations and world events. The easiest of those sources, readily found on the Internet, are those from the U.S. government. We have to remember that the U.S. government reports the conditions and events in other nations, not only with a slight bias, but also in a very cautious way. Many times they overstate difficulties, struggles, or issues in order to ensure that the American reader is "properly warned." If you are an extra-cautious person and an extra-cautious traveler, then the U.S. government informational websites are for you.

Don't get me wrong, I read the websites. I seek as much up-to-date information as is possible, and I bear their information and their warnings in mind. That said, I've never *not* traveled to a country where I've had business because of the warnings offered on these websites. Certainly things like national elections, strikes, or rebellions can influence a trip. That's especially true with regard to our *behavior* once inside that country.

Get an overview of conditions in the part of the world in which you have an interest. As an example, let's say I'm interested in travel in the Caribbean. Had I not traveled in the area, I'd want to get an overview of the area, so that's where I'd start.

May I emphasize? When I read about an area, particularly from government sources—*which I heartily recommend*—I use the information *as a guide only*. It is rare that I heed all of the warnings in such a way as to keep me from going to a locale. I do heed the information as being meaningful, at least to bear in mind, to help me know that a situation or condition exists in that locale and then to be sensitive to it.

So I'm going to travel first to the Caribbean; let's say it's a pleasure cruise. I easily located general information from the end of February 2007, when I was working on this part of the book. (With the sites I recommend, you can be informed within the week of any locale, pretty much throughout the world.)

The information below is from one source only. It is *not* all-inclusive, but I think you'll see how reading it will give you a sense of what's going on there, in general. Remember—*stand back from what you read, and view it as interesting information only*. Even the very, very conservative U.S. State Department isn't warning travelers *not* to go to the Caribbean.

It's interesting to know that in March and April, the 2007 Cricket World Cup will be taking place in the Caribbean.

Players and visitors from all over the world will be coming to the area, and that will change the conditions and experience of the visitor. *Information such as this will be true for almost every place one will travel, at almost any given time.* It's important for us, as Americans, to know that important things are constantly happening in other parts of the world! As a general statement, we don't think like that. Without being accusatory to Americans, we still tend to think in terms of all of life being centered, initiated, and lived best right here, in America. So "CWC," then, refers to the Cricket World Cup. Yes, it would be very, very useful for us to be generally aware that cricket is a big deal ... lots of people love it, and it's a major source of revenue; and that people involved in extraordinary activities in that part of the world might just find us more engaging—may I say "likeable"?—if we show interest in them and their activities. So here we go, then:

Crime

Protection against criminal activity will be the primary day-to-day concern for those traveling to, residing in, or doing business in the Caribbean this spring. High-profile sporting events have historically increased petty and street crime in a host country, with wealthy foreign visitors providing ample targets for robbery and burglary. Crime-related threats OSAC has documented during major international sporting events include: increased reports of demonstrations due to activists using major events as an international stage, increased reports of vandalism, and collateral damage from demonstrations and facilities being directly targeted by anti-globalization activists.

Eastern Caribbean criminals tend to stealthily target residences and lower-end resorts and hotels when the opportunity presents itself. Sometimes weapons are employed. Purse-snatching and pickpocketing commonly occur in high-traffic commercial centers. Police response is generally below North American standards due to inadequate staffing and training, slow response times, and poor deterrence capabilities.

Host nations for the Cricket World Cup can be categorized according to the level of threat from crime. Six countries (Antigua & Barbuda, Barbados, Grenada, St. Kitts & Nevis, St. Vincent and the Grenadines, Saint Lucia) present a moderate threat—mostly from petty and street crime, while three countries (Guyana, Jamaica, Trinidad & Tobago) present a high threat that includes violent crime and significant disruptions from civil unrest. This section provides an overview of the general concerns regarding crime and safety for the Cricket World Cup. References for country-specific information in greater depth can be found at the end of this report.

Moderate Crime Threat

Antigua & Barbuda, Barbados, Grenada, St. Kitts & Nevis, St. Vincent and the Grenadines, Saint Lucia

Crime and Security

Crime in these countries is characterized by petty theft and street crime, where tourists are significant targets of opportunity. Violent crime takes place but tends not to be directed towards tourists. Mugging, purse snatching, and other robberies may occur in areas near hotels, beaches, and restaurants, and other isolated areas, particularly after dark. Visitors should try to secure valuables in a hotel safe and take care to always lock and secure hotel room doors and windows.

High Crime Threat

Guyana, Jamaica, Trinidad & Tobago

Crime and Security

Considerable violent crime and sizable disturbances from civil unrest are not uncommon in these countries. Violent crime can result from armed attacks for theft that escalate to assault when a victim resists, kidnapping, carjacking, sexual assault, and other drug and gang-related activity present in all three countries.

Politically motivated demonstrations in the past have not been directed at U.S. citizens or companies; however, they could present a notable threat to personal security and business operations during the CWC. While nonviolent protests occur on occasion, widespread civil disorder is not typical. However, the CWC tournament presents an opportunity for groups to utilize the high-profile nature of the event to draw greater attention to their causes by causing unrest and civil disturbances. Sugarcane farmers in Trinidad have already proposed a series of protests against the government to coincide with CWC matches unless their grievances are settled before the tournament. Other groups throughout the Caribbean could similarly seize the opportunity to seek attention for their causes by protesting during the CWC.

There are also key issues of specific concern in each country.

Guyana

A murder rate three times higher than that in the United States identifies the serious threat from violent crime in Guyana, including assault, home invasion, kidnapping, and carjacking. Areas of particular caution include the cities of Georgetown and New Amsterdam and transit to and from Cheddi Jagan International Airport, particularly when traveling from dusk to dawn, due to violent attacks that have occurred on the road to the airport. Local law enforcement has been largely ineffectual in coping with the high level of violent crime.

Jamaica

Extreme poverty, gangs, and drugs influence the high rate of violent crime in Jamaica. The greater Kingston area is the most criminally active and dangerous area on the island. Gang violence and shootings occur regularly in certain areas of Kingston and Montego Bay, although predominantly tourist areas are generally free of most violent crime. Crime is exacerbated by the fact that police are understaffed and ineffective.

A factor further influencing the criminal threat in Jamaica will be the presence of American college students visiting on their spring breaks. Jamaica typically attracts approximately 20,000 spring break tourists every year. Although many of the prime resorts are near Montego Bay rather than Kingston, there is still a possibility the overlap could create a dangerous mix of partying college students and cricket fans.

Trinidad & Tobago

Violent crime in Trinidad has increased steadily in recent years, the majority of which is gang/drug related or domestic in nature and is a growing concern for the local security services and the general population. A significant and growing portion of the violence is attributed to the influence of illegal narcotics and firearms. Nonetheless, most crimes occur against victims of opportunity and tend to take place in isolated and high-crime areas. Most reported crimes occur within the metropolitan areas of Port of Spain and San Fernando.

Emergency Preparedness and Medical Conditions

Medical conditions at CWC venue nations are essentially adequate for at least basic treatment, although the influx of visitors during the tournament will certainly strain even the best-prepared locations. Increased demands on services in countries hosting matches may strain not only housing and transportation structures but also emergency medical response and other public services. Sanitation varies by location but is typically below U.S. standards and could contribute to the spread of infectious diseases borne by visitors from around the globe.

Emergency Preparedness

Host nations will be severely tested if they are called upon to implement actions to counter major crowd control, respond to terror attacks, or apply other disaster response planning. These nations do not possess the substantive capabilities in security or medical services that have been observed at other recent major international sporting events. Caribbean police and ambulance services and hospitals may be ill equipped to respond to large-scale emergencies.

Adequate Medical Facilities

Antigua & Barbuda, Barbados, Grenada, Jamaica

These host venues can be described as being equipped with adequate medical facilities and personnel trained to handle routine and immediate emergency care. Medical infrastructure may be able to absorb the increased demands on facilities during the CWC, at least for routine cases and small-scale security/medical incidents. However, large-scale medical emergencies may overwhelm the Jamaican medical facilities.

Jamaica

Although comprehensive emergency services are available in both Kingston and Montego Bay, the general state of medical conditions in Jamaica has been compromised by the first outbreak of malaria in forty years. Since November 30, approximately 170 cases of malaria were confirmed, mostly in highly populated areas. In late January 2007, the Jamaican Health Ministry announced it had halted the outbreak after treatment of all cases and public education. However, since this outbreak occurred so recently, further outbreaks are possible, especially with the arrival of persons from infected areas.

Substandard Medical Facilities

Guyana, St. Kitts & Nevis, Saint Lucia, St. Vincent and the Grenadines, Trinidad & Tobago

Unfortunately, medical conditions at several other host nations are comparatively inadequate, with significant limitations to emergency care and hospitalization due to a shortage of appropriately trained specialists and nurses, below-standard hospital care, and poor sanitation. Ambulance services can be unreliable, and serious medical problems may require evacuation to another island. These nations' medical infrastructure would be severely strained by even moderate-scale security or medical incidents. Operational continuity and contingency planning for these locales may want to assume that only basic medical assistance may be available during the CWC.

TERRORISM

The threat of terrorism during the Cricket World Cup is low. There are no known transnational terrorist groups operating within the Caribbean, although al-Qaeda affiliated organizations have had some interest in conducting attacks against U.S. interests in the area.

Islamist extremist groups have been active on the island of Trinidad in the past: the Jammat al-Muslimeen (JaM) led by Imam Yasin Abu Bakr made a failed coup attempt against the Trinidadian government in 1990. Trinidad and U.S. security forces have placed the JaM, as well as a few other Muslim groups with suspected extremist leanings, under surveillance. The downtown area of Port of Spain experienced four bombings between August 2005 and November 2005. The first of these bombings injured fourteen people, two critically. While no bombings have occurred since November 2005, the perpetrator(s) have not been arrested and the identity and motive of the bomber(s) remains unknown.

The low threat assessment could change if Pakistani President Pervez Musharraf makes good on his promise to attend the Cricket World Cup if Pakistan advances to the semifinals: Islamist terrorists upset with Musharraf's regime have routinely attempted to assassinate him, and the popularity of cricket within Pakistan and India would make the event a high-profile target. Matches between India and Pakistan (which could occur on April 1, 15, 18, or 19 depending on how well the teams do in the group stage) could also make tempting targets for Hindu or Muslim extremists, but this is unlikely.

Cruise ships, yachts, and other pleasure craft present another possible target for a potential terrorist strike. There will be large concentrations of the ships plying the Caribbean during the event, and the host nation naval security forces may be limited in their ability to respond to a hijacking or other method of attack.

A lingering concern among some in both the public and private sectors is that of the West Indies being used as a terrorist transit route to gain entry into the United States. The ten host nations of the Cricket World Cup have joined together to form a 'single domestic space' for the event. Visitors to the World Cup need only secure one common visa, which will allow them to freely move between the host nations. Cricket spectators from Canada, France, Germany, Ireland, Italy, Japan, the Netherlands, South Africa, Spain, the United States of America, and the United Kingdom will not be required to obtain a CWC visa. Most other Caribbean states (excluding Haiti) are also exempted from obtaining a CWC visa.

(Quote from the *Overseas Security Advisory Council Daily Digest*, U.S. Department of State. You may now know that the cricket coach from Pakistan died a mysterious death, at first believed to be a murder; now that conclusion is in question. In spite of this, very little disruption occurred in the Caribbean.)

We *must* rise above the fear that might arise when we read the section on terrorism. How easy it would be to decide not to go, based on that alone!

I first traveled to the Caribbean in the early 1970s. It was a wonderful cruise. With most cruises, one spends most of his or her time on board the ship, traveling among the ports to be visited and virtually never spending the night on shore. On the cruise, I went ashore and spent the day, most of the time touring in areas other than those to which our guides wanted to steer us so we could spend our money. I generally find a taxi to be the best mode of travel, though sometimes a local, personal guide can provide the value-added insights.

Is there something to know about taxis? Sure. Sometimes— very, very rarely, I might add—they are shills for con men, and sometimes they will take you to bad places in an effort to get your money. So how do we protect ourselves from that threat? Avoiding taxis is not the answer. Depending on the country, see if the cab is part of a fleet. Usually one that is part of a fleet has uniform prices and is safe for tourists. Look at the cab. Is it part of a fleet? Is it a mainstream cab? Is it safe and clean looking? (I know, that's a relative term, but you can quickly get a picture of the local standards. In areas where tourists go, there are many cabs, and you can get a feeling for what's average there. Ask the taxi driver how much it will cost for whatever you want to do: go to a specific location, tour for an hour, whatever. He *can* give you a fixed price. What's his attitude and demeanor?

Don't get into a cab with a surly driver! Don't get into a cab with a smarmy, solicitous driver! I probably wouldn't get in with a driver who couldn't communicate rates (written or spoken) or demonstrate that he knew where I wanted to go. (They'll nod their head in response to anything you say!)

Back to my point regarding the Caribbean. I took an afternoon tour of the island of St. Thomas. Most of my other shipmates stayed in the main port, Charlotte Amalie, and shopped. Good fun indeed. Instead, I got a cab. I asked him to drive out of the port town and into the hills. He was very engaging, and he drove slowly and methodically, knowing that I wanted to see what I could in an hour, yet not rushing, so that I could actually *see*. I asked him questions as we went. He explained what he knew. He wasn't a travel guide, and I knew that he was telling me from the perspective of a person who was a local, of one who lived where he was driving. He described some of the abject poverty in the outlying communities. He didn't particularly warn me, but he said, "You don't want to see too much of this. It's really disagreeable." In a sense, he was right. We don't often see whole families living in conditions that would never be allowed in 99 percent of America's communities: tin, wood, and cardboard structures, co-occupied by animals necessary for the existence of the human inhabitants. The driver knew that.

I wasn't shocked by what I saw, but it was indeed disagreeable. I was caught in an environment wherein I—the tourist, the mainstay of this entire community—saw what I was supporting: abject poverty. No, we don't create it. No guilt is meant. We are supporting it in that it is from us that they get most of what they live on. Welfare programs are either very modest or nonexistent in most emerging nations.

I guess it was on that trip that I rethought my ideas about bartering with the locals to get a four-dollar trinket down to three dollars and feeling good about it. Is it somehow different from buying an ounce of Chanel No. 5 tax-free? I think so. Now I can spot an item made locally (not in China, as some are given to sell), give the asking price to that local, and hope that it has somehow actually benefited their community. Do I *really* want to walk away feeling good about having out-bargained an undereducated, struggling local whose price is already dirt cheap?

The point is, conditions are not much different there today than they were thirty-five years ago. Oh, yes, in some ways, things have changed. Maybe evil is a *little* more rampant than it was, but not much. Social disease is kind of like physical disease. Do we really suffer that much more from some of our "popular" diseases? Maybe a little. But isn't it that we now identify them more easily? Or we identify symptoms *very* early (they are present whether we identify them or not), and almost no one dies of natural causes anymore! Such it is with social issues. Our new, small world is made small by virtue of electronic media and the much, much greater ease of reporting happenings around the globe.

Okay, maybe when I went to the Caribbean in the early 1970s, there wasn't a Cricket World Cup that would artificially draw many more people. But there *were* the usual issues happening that I simply didn't read about in advance. I didn't know that I "needed" to be frightened! So I wasn't.

To summarize, read about the place to which you will travel. Tourism sites and literature are fine for getting a certain feel for what to expect. Of course, they will color the information. That color may or may not lead to an inaccurate view of the place. So it is with government information. It's colored … it's slanted. With both views, there is something to be heard, something to be learned. Do I *not* travel to Aruba because "they are kidnapping and killing tourists"? Of course not! Be wise as you read reports that characterize a society because of an infamous deed. Similarly, the message "go to Tasco (Mexico) for good buys of silver products" is true, essentially. But once there, we'll encounter all kinds of product qualities, and we'll need to exercise good common sense.

Chapter 3
It's All in the Preparation

Attitude

In the last chapter, I emphasized a few things:

1) We Americans are just waking up to what the rest of the world knows and has been living with for years.

2) We are seeing how the rest of the world views us … and why (in spite of the popularity of the book *The Ugly American*).

3) Overall, the huge, huge majority of the world is kindly toward us.

This becomes a segue into this larger section on preparation, which is led by a discussion on attitude.

I had to decide about my attitude for a trip I was making to Paraguay. Here is the setup. Paraguay has one of the world's largest underground economies related to counterfeit products. Little Paraguay. We were hired to investigate counterfeit products being imported into Paraguay, then being repackaged or "re-manufactured" and subsequently exported to points all over the world.

Stick with me through this explanation. It's amazing stuff.

Here's Paraguay:

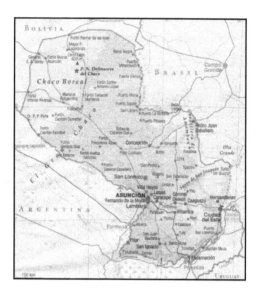

It's pretty much landlocked—not totally, as I'll explain. Listen to what an official U.S. State Department document says about Paraguay:

> Landlocked Paraguay has a market economy marked by a large informal sector. This sector features both reexport of imported consumer goods to neighboring countries, as well as the activities of thousands of microenterprises and urban street vendors. Because of the importance of the informal sector, accurate economic measures are difficult to obtain. A large percentage of the population derives its living from agricultural activity, often on a subsistence basis. The formal economy grew by an average

of about 3 percent annually in 1995–97 but averaged near-zero growth in 1998–2001 and contracted by 2.3 percent in 2002, in response to regional contagion and an outbreak of hoof-and-mouth disease. On a per capita basis, real income has stagnated at 1980 levels. Most observers attribute Paraguay's poor economic performance to political uncertainty, corruption, lack of progress on structural reform, substantial internal and external debt, and deficient infrastructure. (*CIA Factbook,* February 9, 2007)

May I explain the "large informal sector" of the market economy? No, on second thought, lest you doubt the information, this is from a travel book, *Argentina, Uruguay & Paraguay* (Wayne Bernhardson, Lonely Planet, 1999, page 767). Here, the discussion is about the city where our investigation centered. It is called Ciudad del Este ("City of the East"). Look at the map. Its name is right below Asunción.

Formerly Puerto Presidente Stroessner, Ciudad del Este is a key border crossing, a transportation hub, and one of the gateways to the world-famous Cataratas del Iguazú. It is perhaps more significant, in the words of the *Wall Street Journal,* as the site of "15,000 shops jammed into twenty blocks, a chaos of mass consumption that turns over up to U.S. $55 billion per year in contraband—five times the size of the official Paraguayan economy.

Fifteen thousand shops, $55 billion. Here is some perspective about that illegal economy. It is five times the official Paraguayan economy. Let me hearken back to the State Department document cited above. That document provides several gross domestic product figures for Paraguay. This first is the GDP for purchasing power parity: $30.64 billion.

This entry gives the gross domestic product (GDP) or value of all final goods and services produced within a nation in a

Ciudad del Este aerial

given year. A nation's GDP at purchasing power parity (PPP) exchange rates is the sum value of all goods and services produced in the country valued at prices prevailing in

the United States. This is the measure most economists prefer when looking at per-capita welfare and when comparing living conditions or use of resources across countries.

The next is the GDP for the official exchange rate, which is $ 7.696 billion.

> The measure is simple to compute and gives a precise measure of the value of output. Many economists prefer this measure when gauging the economic power an economy maintains vis-à-vis its neighbors, judging that an exchange rate captures the purchasing power a nation enjoys in the international marketplace *(CIA World Factbook,* February 9, 2007).

$7.696 billion ... that's the working GDP for the whole country! The "large informal sector," with a figure of $55 billion in 1999, is just about eight times the GDP of the entire country. Here's what all of that means: eight times the nation's GDP in unofficial revenue is produced in Ciudad del Este each year. Folks, it's illegal activity, and it is substantially untaxed.

Okay, so now I know that there is an enclave of crime awaiting us, and it's no small potatoes, either! Knowing all of this, how does one prepare to go to such an area? Mentally and emotionally, I mean. Well, to be quite honest, I didn't know all of this before my first trip. I learned all of this while we were there and while we were working. Oh, I knew that the area in which we were trying to work produced an estimated $55 billion a year and that that amount was eight times the GDP of Paraguay. I didn't have a clue about what that *meant*, and I didn't have an understanding about the significance of the businesses there. What I did learn was that about 300,000 people live in Ciudad del Este. Of that number, it is estimated that there are approximately 40,000 Middle Eastern inhabitants. It is publicly known that there is substantial support from that Middle Eastern population for Hezbollah and other admitted terrorist groups. Many (most?..) of the 15,000 referenced shops in that area are owned by Middle Easterners.

Over the next few years, we investigated successfully, conducted raids and seizures, supervised arrests, and accomplished our anti-counterfeiting goals. We work very closely with both United States and Paraguayan government officials. I recorded hours of videos of our activities and took hundreds of photographs.

One of the ways merchandise gets in is via the river system. A couple of major rivers—the Paraná, on the east, and the Paraguay, on the west—converge and make their way south as one river, the Rio de la Plata, which dumps into the Atlantic, in the great harbor of Montevideo, Uruguay, and Buenos Aires, Argentina. Deep-water craft can and do negotiate that waterway, bringing goods, usually through the Panama Canal, from China. Huge, huge business. So much for "landlocked"!

Back to Attitude

So now what's my attitude going to be as I go to visit and work there, given this brief amount of information that you now have? Illegal activity is *the* huge business. Strong terrorist financing is derived from the profits, and there's some government corruption.

Think about that.

Listen, you may not feel comfortable going to a place like that, given that information. My point isn't to talk you into going someplace that you deem to be dangerous, or to act foolishly ... not at all. There's a number of good investigators who simply won't go there. You have to make your own decisions. What I'm encouraging you to do here, by using a rather extreme example, is to get you to think about how *you* make your decisions about whether to go or not to go. And if you *do* go, how will you approach your venture? Every place in this world is a place where some people would rather not go, for one reason or another ... right?

How do you make your decision about whether to travel or not? I'd suggest it's substantially based on your attitude, especially your attitude about people.

Whether you are conscious of it or not, you make a series of decisions. Let's eliminate an important one: money. Can I afford it or not? Personally, I think cost is a non-issue. I also think that whether the attractions in an area are "big enough" is also not an issue, only because that is so very subjective. In my opinion, there aren't many places on this Earth that *aren't* worth visiting. I'd say it all comes down to this question: *Is it worth the time and the effort to go?* And I think all the component parts of *that* decision boil down to this: *What do I think about people?*

Think about it. Here are some considerations and objections:

- I don't speak the language.
- I'm concerned (afraid?) about finding my way around (making connections, going from place to place, etc.).
- I'm unfamiliar with or uncomfortable with the customs (dress, food, habits).
- I don't want to stand in lines or be hustled around at a tourist attraction. (Do you remember that you likely *will* have to "deal with people" if you go to a tourist attraction?)

Stop for a moment. Ask yourself this question. Really. Consider this carefully:

What do you think about people?

Does that sound like a silly question? I don't think so.

In order to get to that answer, consider this: When someone mentions doing something that involves people, what's the first thing that comes to mind? Your work associate says, "I'm going to the ball game on Saturday." Is your first thought about enjoying a ball game? Or do you react to the thought of the crowd, of fighting the traffic? Is the crowd at a ball game part of the enjoyment? Or is watching it on TV better, given the option?

Someone mentions flying from the East Coast to, say, San Francisco. Or Boston. Or Jacksonville. Or New Orleans. Or Denver. Or Los Angeles ... or Asunción. Let's put aside the financial difficulty one might have in doing that. What is your first reaction to the concept? Do what I would call "little obstacles" rise up and override the adventure of the travel and of meeting people? Don't get me wrong. Invariably I am distracted by consideration of the logistics if I go anyplace farther than the grocery store. But we want that distraction to be temporary and minor, in comparison with the excitement that should arise when we know that a trip is ahead of us.

Do you *realize* how many individuals believe that people are a bother? That people get in the way? I've actually heard individuals say, "This world is fine except for the people." Some parents say they just can't wait until their children are grown and gone. (They don't know what they're saying!) How many people do you know who hate their jobs (most, it seems to me)? Invariably, when you get into any kind of conversation with them about it, it's about the people.

Let me tell you how many people outside the United States view us. One of the people with whom I spoke in Latin America was a translator and a court reporter: an educated woman. We got onto the subject of American culture and American behavior. Eventually she told me that her primary view of American society was based on things she saw on television. It's probably not an unreasonable way to get information about America, right? Don't we form our own views about most of our lives based on what we see or read or hear in the media? It turns out she mostly watched crime and drama stories on TV. She believed that the drug culture had a very strong presence in American life. While that's true at one level, for the average American, life in the United States is *not* about constant drug trade and shootings. But that was her honest view of us.

Here's something else that most people outside of the USA know about us. They know that one of our major pastimes is taking each other to court and suing one another. In fact, the United States may be the most litigious nation on Earth. Several years ago I read a statistic from the US Dept of Justice Bureau of Statistics, that said that each year, enough lawsuits are filed that one in eight adults could be involved in one. Of course, that's a statistic that includes the many, many lawsuits involving single entities such as highly vulnerable corporations.

So in actuality, we won't see one in every eight adults sued. But the point is, we're suing everybody. I've worked on complex business-law cases in which sons are suing fathers. I had one case in which a large recreational-vehicle distributor was owned by a family that had been operating the business for decades. A dispute arose between the father and the sons. The result was that a large family of sons, daughters, cousins, wives, and in-laws was destroyed. What is that? It could've been about money; it could've been about principles; it could've been jealousy, control, or just plain greed. But in any event, the result was that people were less important than whatever their particular "presenting problem" was.

There are elements of truth in those two views (drugs and lawsuits), aren't there? And yet they don't define the vast majority of Americans, do they? There are probably three or four other major concepts that people have about us Americans. How do we categorize the citizens of other nations? Are the British cold and standoffish? Are the Germans rock-jawed, stubborn, and arrogant? Are the Irish drinkers, the Italians lovers, the French …?

Is that you? If you can honestly say yes, don't feel bad. We all make gross generalizations. If you are a person who occasionally makes choices based on wanting to avoid crowds, don't think that makes you a sociopath. We all have preferences. That's good. For instance, I'm a person who (at least for the last forty or so years) has said no to regular requests to go to large-crowd sporting events.

Just be aware of your thinking on these kinds of subjects about people, and be willing to consider changing or at least taking in new information to challenge your old thinking patterns.

I didn't ask that question to be mean or to dredge up old, hard feelings. But the answer to that question is going to be very useful to you as you consider your travel, whether business or pleasure, and whether in the confines of the United States or into foreign countries.

How will you make your plans if your view of life is that people are out to get you? I thought that way. I have some idea of how one plans when he thinks that way. You make your plans based on a fear of people trying to take advantage of you, as compared to the joy of being able to meet new people and to expect the best of adventure. Now, stop right there! Don't get the idea that the plans I'm going to mention aren't good things to consider. What I'm saying is that if you make plans *based* on the thinking that people are out to get you, your whole trip is going to be affected.

So what's an example of that? Years ago, when I was taking an international trip, I began to hear a lot of stories about how in that area there were a lot of thieves and pickpockets and that snatch-and-grab crimes took place with regularity. I can't tell you how many hours of preparation time—and more importantly, mental anguish—were expended prior to traveling, in an effort to safeguard against those threats (or rumored or imagined threats).

I bought the secret-wallet-under-the-shirt device; I made sure that I had virtually no cash and only traveler's checks; I put a comb sideways through my wallet in my rear pocket so that it couldn't be grabbed out easily. I must've provided lots of entertainment for the local people as I tried to get out my wallet and got my comb hung up on the pocket edges ... not to speak of the fact that I had almost no money in the darn thing.

What else have I done? I've researched every possible health problem that a foreign country has ever encountered. I considered whether or not to get the dozens of inoculations that would have (perhaps) protected me. Wisdom and proper research will tell you when to get the inoculations. As I've mentioned, it's been more than a decade since I've gotten any inoculations whatsoever. This is not—repeat, *not*—a recommendation against inoculations!

More? Sure. When I traveled to countries where the consumption of water was a potential hazard, once again I got into so much research that in the end, I was more confused than I was educated. I checked with health specialists, I read research papers, and last—sadly, I chose to do what was most important last —I spoke to veteran travelers of the area. Once again, the research can be extremely valuable. However, I found that when I spoke with people who had traveled extensively, or even lived in the area, they provided the most helpful information.

On trips, I've taken my own water purification systems, I've taken water purification tablets, and to be perfectly honest, I never used any of it. I've never had a problem. What you find out is that if there is such a problem, whether it be water or food—or bandits—the locals are going to be able to help with good advice.

Here's the deal. Overwhelmingly, the citizens of every country that you and I would consider visiting are good, loving people who have families and friends and put their pants on one leg at a time, just like we do. Whether we're traveling or not, every person—repeat after me—every person has something valuable to tell us. Add that fact to another truth, which is that most of the people whom we encounter will be service professionals, individuals who provide a service to others. They know that their performance is going to determine their compensation, to a large extent. So what we are going to encounter is friendly people who *want to do good for us*, not harm. They'll help us, not hurt us.

Many times, in foreign countries, a person's individual services are negotiable. Here's a simple example of that. When I got off the airplane at the very small airport at Iguazú Falls, Brazil, I was stormed by men and boys (sorry, no females) who wanted to carry my bags. Most of them don't have baggage carts; they carry them. So I generally look for a person who has a smile and is large enough to handle my luggage. There is no fee established for that help, and in the instance of Brazil and most Latin countries, the porter is totally at the mercy of the traveler to decide how much he will be compensated.

There are no unions, and they are not in uniforms. They don't even have anything like our "dollar or two dollars per bag" starting point. Sure, in a hotel, particularly in a fancier hotel, you might feel like the baggage boy expects to receive the kind of money that we pay in the United States, but I've observed a couple of things. I'm sad to say that Americans, more than any other group, tend to get a look of fear on their faces when they see the mostly little bodies descending upon them. It's tragic humor to see an American mother pull her small children next to her when the local boys come near. Second, I see these same people struggling mightily under the weight of their own luggage, sometimes for hundreds of yards, when, for two dollars, they could've been relieved of their burden and could have blessed the local economy.

One more vignette: while I can tell you that I've never lost any luggage, I have encountered a few flight problems and schedule changes. For some reason, it seems like if there is going to be some change or confusion, it comes in São Paulo, Brazil. São Paulo is something of a connection hub for South America.

My flight to Asunción, Paraguay, had been delayed, and there was a crowd around the airline desk. Sadly, once again, the most vocal and most verbal complainants were English speakers. Don't get me wrong; I'm not about bashing Americans or English speakers. As you know, the ticket people really have little to do with whether a flight leaves or does not, and they are almost never about trying to personally punish us in some way by not letting the flight go. (Somehow, some people think they are.) In this instance, I noticed something. It was a cultural thing.

It struck me that, as a gross generalization, Latins have a different approach to lines than Americans do. Latins will queue up … and we queue up too. If something or someone is holding up the line, for the most part, we will not break out of that line for almost anything. Our positions in that line are *ours* … forever. Irrevocably. Not to move. Never give it up.

Latins, on the other hand, will break line with the least provocation. A change of personnel at the ticket counter, a change of the flight marquee … about anything will give them permission to push forward as a crowd to the ticket counter and begin to verbalize their cases. Only rarely have I seen them actually shout or in any way even approach getting ugly in their questioning. And that seems to be the big difference. They tend to question, and we tend to accuse. We are orderly and don't break the line, and we will speak out freely in a loud and often offensive tone, without shame. Don't get me wrong; neither way works particularly well.

What I've learned, and what is exemplified in this vignette that has happened to me many times, is that if my *attitude* is to believe that the ticket agent is probably more interested in getting things straightened out than even I am, then I can approach the whole issue with patience. And that is what is true!

Do we actually think they *enjoy* seeing an angry crowd in front of them? In most of those situations, a patient attitude can make a person a standout in a very positive way. I can't tell you how many times a ticket agent has noticed me standing in the middle of a line, waiting patiently, and called me over to his position to take care of me. I can't recall the last time that I totally missed a flight or didn't get to where I need to go pretty much as planned.

Attitude.

Thoughts

Remember: No one is looking over your shoulder. Do an attitude check. Think about it.

- What *do* you think about people?
- Do you *like* them?
- Is life about "me against them"?
- Are non-Americans "children of a lesser god"?
- Do you have negative, preconceived notions about travel?
- Would you actually prefer traveling in a bubble to having to put up with the people and the crowds?

Consider these questions and concepts. I think we all struggle with some of those thoughts at times. Be aware of that, that's all.

When you go forward, go forward expecting the best. You'll attract the best if you do. If you bear these things in mind, it will completely change both the preparation and the outcome of your trip.

Chapter 4
Learning

Continuing in Preparation

I have to admit it.

I've *really* come to enjoy doing a little research about an area into which I'm going to venture. It wasn't always like that.

You've had to do those long, dry social-studies or history projects when you were in school, probably junior high? You know the ones. You had to look up all the nations of the United Nations, and then you had to go to the library; next, you had to make a card for each country. For us, in the days before computers, that card was a five-by-eight index card. On that card were the major topics for research on that country, with some space after each major category. The categories might be something like geography, people, government, economy, politics, military, transportation, customs, health care/actuaries, etc. Then

45

you'd have three-by-five cards, and each of the cards would have information about each of the individual topics. We put all the cards together and wrote a short report about the country. Boy, I hated those projects!

Now, years later ... hey! Those classes and that research turns out to be almost as valuable as my high-school typing class. When you're going someplace, you may not need to do that kind of extensive project. But like me, you may end up wanting to. Now, with the Internet, it's much faster, although I think the reliability of the information is a bit more questionable. Nonetheless, as I've mentioned before, we're going to take the information we receive into consideration but not allow it to totally rule any part of our decision making.

Where do *I* start?

Learn Some General Information

I like to go first to the local newspaper, either one in the city to which I'm traveling or to a city close by. This link is a great start: http://library.uncg.edu/news/. In the United States, this link is excellent too: http://www.onlinenewspapers.com/; it has international links too, but for the United States, I prefer it. There are often English-speaking versions available, if you're going to a country where English is not the primary language.

This might be an opportune time to remind you that English is now the established and accepted business language of the world. That means that when I've been in a country whose native language I did not speak (I speak English and Spanish), I've never been more than two or three people removed from someone who speaks English. I'm not saying that to strengthen or encourage our overall lack of interest in speaking other languages but rather to enable you to rest assured that speaking the local language is usually not a requirement. *I can't overemphasize* that being able to speak the local language will completely change and improve your experience there. Later I'm going to talk a little bit about the value of learning even just a few words or a short phrase or two.

Next, go to Wikipedia (http://en.wikipedia.org/wiki/ Country_list). You can be there in a few seconds, and you'll find this wonderful list of countries, as of my writing current from February 27, 2007. It will look like this:

South America

- Argentina — Buenos Aires
- Bolivia — Sucre (seat of government at La Paz)
- Brazil — Brasília
- Chile — Santiago
- Colombia — Bogotá
- Ecuador — Quito
- *Falkland Islands* (overseas territory of the United Kingdom) — Stanley
- *French Guiana* (overseas department of France) — Cayenne
- Guyana — Georgetown
- Paraguay — Asunción
- Peru — Lima
- Suriname — Paramaribo
- Uruguay — Montevideo
- Venezuela — Caracas

A click on the country of your choice results in a pretty significant amount of general information, usually a small map, a copy of the flag (as you can see), and some very good beginning information. And may I comment? Wikipedia is not the source to use if you're doing serious research or working on your PhD. Everyone knows that the accuracy of the information is often questionable. But for our purposes here, it's a great place to at least start. Just consider what is illustrated here, in this short list. Believe me, if travelers have just this amount of information, obtainable in just a few minutes, printed or put on their PDAs, and read it over for a minute or two while on the plane, that alone really enhances the traveling experience.

Everyone's heard about the nation of Abkhazia, right? Not! But see the kind of information that is available just on Wikipedia about that nation:

1. Political Status
2. Geography and climate
3. Economy
4. Demographics
5. History
   a. Early history
   b. Abkhazia within the Russian Empire and Soviet Union
   c. The Abkhazian War
   d. De jure Government of Abzhazia
6. Politics
7. International involvement
8. Gallery of Abkhazia
9. Notes
10. External links

I don't want to sound melodramatic here, but do you have any idea how rare it is that anyone travels to a foreign country with even the remotest amount of information about the country to which they're traveling? It's really rare.

Sure, there may be educational tours or a certain few individuals who know about the area, but that's unusual. Even the very few times I've used the services of a guide (and I'm not discouraging the use of a guide at all), if *I've* known information about the area, it has really contributed to my experience and sometimes the experience of others in my company.

I've had hundreds of encounters with foreign people in their countries, and I can't remember a time when they weren't surprised, if not amazed, when I expressed interest in them or their country by knowing even just a little bit of information.

I'm serious. I've even seen expressions of shock on a person's face when I told him that I'm aware of a particular national holiday in his country, for instance. Or, heaven forbid, if I were to know about a strike in that country at the time!

Latin countries have more holidays than Carter has liver pills. (Does that phrase date me?) It's really pretty cool. We (who, by the way, observe about twelve different national holidays) might think that the twenty or thirty national holidays in a foreign country are excessive. They aren't lazy; they enjoy celebrating. We Americans, who scoff at all those holidays, enjoy hanging around the water cooler while being "on the clock."

Western European—more specifically, American—business habits have really changed the business habits of Latin America. Many, especially larger, businesses observe the kinds of business hours that American companies observe, especially institutions such as banks, the postal service, and some large corporations. That said, you will still find a heavy hearkening back to the Latin tradition of starting the workday a little later; taking a later, longer lunch hour; and ending the workday at a later hour. Yes, it's true: restaurants will still be quite empty as late as 9:00 PM each evening. Get-down-to-it dining really starts at about 10 PM.

On the other hand, if you're simply hungry, and if you want to eat in a fine restaurant, haven't made a reservation, and don't need to be social, you can go to almost any fine restaurant at, say, 8:00 PM, and walk in finding the place virtually empty. You will be told they are open, and they will seat you and feed you as if you were the most important customer of the day. If they're just beginning to prepare their kitchen, it may take just a little bit longer to receive your food ... but they don't wave you away. I have *never* found a CLOSED sign on the front of a foreign restaurant in which workers were preparing to start their day. As a matter of kindness, grace, and good business, they will virtually always serve you.

On one trip to Argentina, I was there during the week of national elections. Because of that, certain opposing parties were trying to make their last-minute political points. Organized labor decided to protest the current government by making several piles of automobile tires and lighting them on fire in the middle of boulevards. Doesn't that conjure up images of open street rioting and murder?

I knew in advance about the national elections because I had read ahead. I mentioned to one of the individuals with whom I was meeting that I was aware that there were national elections, and they told me that the protests would occur and explained how the government reacts. What I saw was kind of like in the movies.

Many or most Latin countries rely on their military to do what the police departments do in the United States. So you saw the protesters throwing tires on the burning heap, and all around, up and down the boulevard, were soldiers with automatic weapons. No big deal. *That's the way they do things.* If you weren't aware of that, and if you saw that whole drama take place, it might cause you to take refuge in your hotel and catch the earliest flight out.

While not wanting to diminish the plight of any particular group, the dynamic is pretty interesting. Paper abounds during protests. They are still very much into printing up and distributing flyers and pamphlets, and it seems like trillions of them are strewn during a protest, and the next day, they're gone. Much of the time, that's accomplished by individual laborers. Some of the more metropolitan cities utilize modern machinery to do this work, but from trash collection to cleanup, the most utilized machinery by far is human labor.

In Buenos Aires, older buildings were constructed with metal shutters. Those shutters can be controlled from inside, and they were designed specifically for protest and rebellion protection. It saves on glass replacement! Again, knowing this, and finding out that any kind of action that even remotely looks like violence occurs rarely, is really useful.

If all you hear is that violent protest is going on in Buenos Aires, you might decide to not go at all. That would be a mistake most of the time. You would miss wonderful, happy people ... who prepare and eat great food, love to dance, and enjoy family life in this city.

Learn a Custom or Two

In Argentina, Uruguay, Paraguay, and Brazil, and to a slightly lesser extent, other Latin countries, they partake in a hot tea drink known as maté (pronounced mah-tay). It's an extremely common folk drink. One of the interesting features about drinking maté is that these countries continue to partake in the ceremonial aspects of it that go back hundreds, if not thousands of years. The drink itself comes from the plant called yerba mate *(Ilex paraguariensis)*. Pretty interesting, eh? I'm telling you this not to bore you but to give an example of how easy and fun it is ... and how meaningful to them.

Traditionally it is cooked and then consumed from a gourd or horn, using a silver straw with a bowl on the bottom with holes to strain the water as it's drunk.

One of the fun parts is that the gourd is shared. Sometimes a small group will be standing around, socializing, and they pass the gourd from one person to the next.

Sharing yerba mate

There is an unwritten code that says if you're ill, you don't partake.

The custom is so strong that when we go on raids, there is a designated thermos and maté person. He carries around the thermos, often housed in a case such as that seen in the photos. *All* individuals are offered the choice to sip.

Good guys, bad guys … all have their maté. Do you remember my mentioning a case in Argentina wherein two tractor-trailers were stolen from a distribution center? The suspects drove up to the security guard shack and asked the guards if they could fill their maté thermos with hot water. The guards allowed them into the guardhouse to do so and were taken captive.

That breach of trust and confidence in a very deeply embedded custom of sharing may have been an even deeper crime than the theft of the property. There really was a look of shock on the faces of the local police and on the faces of the corporate security people when they related the story.

What an ice breaker it was to know this information. And as a bonus, I've developed quite a taste for maté. Yerba mate is priced like coffee; the gourds cost from a few dollars up. The silver straws, called *bombillas*, cost three dollars and up. The gourd (also called the maté) lasts for a long time, but it may eventually crack, and then it must be replaced.

I got to know an attorney in Paraguay who did work for us on behalf of a corporation that we were representing. He introduced me to some of the finer points about yerba mate tea. As I grew to enjoy it, we entered into a new level of friendship, and on one of my trips, I was presented with my own leather-covered thermos, gourd, and *bombilla*.

While walking the streets of any of those countries, you can see bankers, businessmen, housewives, students, and even beggars carrying their maté gourds and straws. During any trip or event that takes longer than about half an hour (about the time to consume one gourd's amount of tea), out comes the thermos in order to carry more hot water.

My maté setup

One of the things that is useful to know about this custom, besides learning to enjoy the tea, is that each of the provinces/states/departments has its own customary design

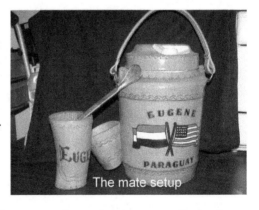

The mate setup

for the gourd. You don't necessarily need to learn anything about those designs, but in knowing that information, for a few dollars, you can honor your contact with a gourd from his region or from a region that he enjoys.

If you know *any* of these kinds of local custom or about pride in a particular kind of product in advance of your trip, you can ask one of the local people where to see or buy that particular product. *That shows an interest in them and their country.* It's an honor thing. That kind of information is virtually always available in even the most basic books or Internet sources.

A fine general information source (though perhaps not always up to date) is one of the Frommer publications. (See Tips page 58.) You can learn if an area is proud of its glass, lace, leather clothing, shoes, or jewelry ... you get the idea. *Doing something like that can be very, very easy and inexpensive.* It can speak volumes about your attitude.

Learn Even a Little about the Country Itself

Look how packed full of information this small paragraph about Brazil is, and consider how many conversations or questions can be generated from it:

> Following three centuries under the rule of Portugal, Brazil became an independent nation in 1822 and a republic in 1889. By far the largest and most populous country in South America, Brazil overcame more than half a century of military intervention in the governance of the country when in 1985 the military regime peacefully ceded power to civilian rulers. Brazil continues to pursue industrial and agricultural growth and development of its interior. Exploiting vast natural resources and a large labor pool, it is today South America's leading economic power and a regional leader. Highly unequal income distribution remains a pressing problem *(CIA World Factbook,* February 9, 2007).

Add to that this map ...

... and now you have an idea of where the major cities are and their relationships to one another, and you can see how very many countries border Brazil. Why, it might even be easy to see that that big blank territory in the middle of the country is probably sparsely inhabited and very likely jungle! You can immediately know where the world-famous Rio de Janeiro is; you can see where the huge cities of São Paulo and Santos are; and by seeing that zero-latitude line just north of the city of Belem, you can know something about the weather and temperature.

Check this out! A State Department document (yes, CIA again) says this about Brazil and the tri-border area to which I previously referred, especially at the Ciudad del Este location. (Find Curitiba in Brazil, just to the left of the *C.*)

(An) unruly region at (the) convergence of Argentina-Brazil-Paraguay borders is (a) locus of money laundering, smuggling, arms and illegal narcotics trafficking, and fundraising for extremist organizations (U.S. Department of State, *CIA World Factbook*, February 9, 2007).

Boy, are those words the *height* of political correctness!

Now here's some bonus information. The recent movie release *Miami Vice* was reviewed on July 28, 2006, by Kenneth Turan of the *LA Times*. Read part of his review (Mann is the writer/director):

> Clearly Mann did a formidable amount of research into the habits of undercover agents and drug smugglers alike, and the film goes to the far corners of South America, including Ciudad del Este at the intersection of Paraguay, Brazil, and Argentina, in its search for authenticity.

Yes, the movie makers paid large, large dollars to people in Ciudad del Este, one of the largest terrorist fund-raising sources, for rights and privileges while filming!

All of that said, just be aware of the sources of information that you consult. I can readily tell you horror stories about every Latin American country. Think about that. Think about your own city. Most of us live in cities where we could focus on the negative about our own living environment and that would warn just about anybody not to visit.

If you do just a little homework, you'll dazzle yourself with how well you do with the people who live in the area you're visiting. That results in *much* greater fun for everyone.

Learn a Word or a Phrase in the Language of the Area You're Visiting

Do you realize that you probably already know a few words of many of the languages of the world? I suspect that if you stop and think about it, you will realize that you do. What becomes difficult—and I think especially for Americans—is risking using those words in the presence of native speakers. I can promise you that I have *never* encountered any person, with whom I tried speaking even just a word or two, who didn't respond very positively. They did not mock or in any way discourage, but almost always showed great pleasure in the fact that I even tried. (We may tend to assume that *they* mock because *we* mock ... whole comedy routines are geared around mocking the way a foreigner sounds as he attempts to speak English.)

Let me mention something else. I would include learning customs and vocabulary for areas right in the United States. Here are two things to think about:

1. You don't want to go into an area of your own country and either laugh at the locals or get angry because "they don't speak English"!

2. Just as we have Southern accents and Northeastern accents (aren't those the only two?), foreign countries have different accents. For instance, look at the choices I have for my Spanish keyboard (Microsoft Windows option):

Spanish	(Argentina)
Spanish	(Bolivia)
Spanish	(Chile)
Spanish	(Colombia)
Spanish	(Dominican Repub)
Spanish	(Ecuador)
Spanish	(El Salvador)
Spanish	(Guatemala)
Spanish	(Honduras)
Spanish	(International Sort)
Spanish	(México)
Spanish	(Nicaragua)
Spanish	(Panama)
Spanish	(Paraguay)
Spanish	(Peru)
Spanish	(Puerto Rico)
Spanish	(Traditional Sort)
Spanish	(Uruguay)
Spanish	(Venezuela)

Don't be daunted. I chose the traditional sort, but that list exists because of the differences among the different "Spanishes"; I don't understand or hear those differences, and in spite of this, I get along fine in all those countries.

You see, knowing just that above gives me additional confidence when traveling and speaking in Spanish areas. I know, now from experience, that even native Spanish speakers sometimes struggle with their own language. Think about our own English—British English, American English, Canadian, Australian, English around the world—and then combine that with Southern U.S. English and all the dialects therein. It takes me a day or two to get my ears acclimated to Alabama English. Can you think of native speakers, perhaps only miles from you, whom you have difficulty understanding?

Tip

Frommer, found at www.frommer.com

Chapter Five
Not All People Think Like Americans
(and "Why is that?" or "What's wrong with them?")

Does it seem like we Americans don't always have the smoothest time outside of our own borders? It's probably true to a large extent; there are probably many reasons for that, and I think we can do a lot to improve or smooth out our visiting and travel experiences outside of our borders. (And probably inside, too.)

This may be something of a philosophy chapter, and it's definitely just my opinion. I offer it not to convince you to think one way or another but rather to ask you to think about these things. Ask yourself where you are on some of this, and realize that we Americans do *not* have a corner on morals, ethics, or values.

Don't get me wrong. I enjoy and prefer most of what we think. But contrary to popular thinking (sometimes of those *outside* of the United States too) the sun neither rises nor sets only in the United States.

There are a number of things unique to Americans, and they help to explain our thinking. Not too many people in this world, outside of the United States, think like Americans.

The United States of America was discovered, founded, and established by adventurous, independent-thinking individuals. Knowing anything about our history tells us that the discoverers and founders were not independent of their native or sponsoring countries, but after having been given the assignment (and funds) to discover and explore, they exercised a great deal of independent and free thinking in doing so.

The emphasis for the first hundred years or so was upon the East Coast of the United States. It wasn't long, however, before exploration and discovery spread west. When you look at a map of the United States, it's pretty easy to see that the states tend to be smaller on the East Coast and larger as they go west. Americans tend to think big and to think expansively.

States' rights (meaning an emphasis on local government) is another established and solid part of American thinking. Our constitution, Bill of Rights, and other constitutional amendments all very carefully established and preserve individual rights, and the intention is that there be a light oversight and participation by the federal government. That's not the *usual* way in the rest of the world.

We call ourselves a democracy when in fact, we are a representative republic but have the mental attitude of being a democracy. That kind of means we think we have individual say, but in fact, we've given our political individualism to the representatives we choose—even though most of us don't know those people's names! Capitalism is the economic underpinning of our country, and that means competition in the marketplace, which may be unparalleled in the rest of the world.

None of this is to say that there aren't problems, sometimes even significant problems. What I've tried to point out here is that there is an attitude, now multiple generations and hundreds of years old, that exalts free thinking, independence, and self-determination.

Along with that—some would say as a natural result—comes a certain amount of self-centeredness, selfishness, and an increasing diminishing of community. Again, consider the significance of the fact that *statistically* enough lawsuits are filed each year that each of us will be sued once every eight years!

Simultaneously, we have crafted our lives to be increasingly *dependent* on our institutions to such a degree that we really have all but given up most of our true independence. We can no longer do without our cell phones, our televisions, or our automobiles; we might suffer a national paralysis if any one of those conveniences was suddenly taken away from us. While we may have one of the best health care systems, we're also one of the least healthy nations. Yes, we may live longer than most, and we also *depend* upon our drug companies to do for us what healthy eating and exercise *could* do for us.

We've gotten used to walking very little; we've crafted our lives to do as little physical work as possible, right down to the dozens and dozens of convenience products in and around our homes to reduce the effort of living. We *depend* upon our toys. I'm including myself.

If you watched the movie *Babel*, especially those segments related to Brad Pitt and Cate Blanchett, did you notice how the tourists on the bus are? And how they are off the bus? Been there, done that. The idea is that we drive along, go through the desert, stop at prearranged tourist spots (even the quaint cafe), and move as a group; the locals are observed. It's kind of like we are in a bubble and never interact with people. You may as well watch a movie. That's not unique to Americans, by any means. I'm not criticizing tours, buses, or people who take them. Look at us from the locals' viewpoint.

I've taken my share of bus tours. It's great—an efficient and economical way to see a lot. My view changed, however, when I took a mission trip to the Dominican Republic, and my thinking about travel—about interacting with people, rather than just viewing them—changed. Once again, I admit that this is a very different trip from either a business trip or the typical pleasure trip. I'm *not* saying any one is better than the other (although if you *really* want to interact with the people of any country, take a mission trip).

While there, our group mingled with people on the streets and in the neighborhoods, and perhaps for the first time I engaged some older people in conversation. I found that they very naturally and spontaneously asked us to come to their homes. We went with them, about fifty yards from where they were standing. It was one of the most modest homes I had ever been in. It had a dirt floor, and I didn't see any exterior windows. They had a television, and the cord was connected to an overhead public utility wire that was strung from one pole to another, and someone had simply spliced the cord into the overhead wire.

We talked for some time, and they told me a little bit about their lives and then asked me about mine. As I was getting ready to leave, the lady of the house picked up what surely must have been their entire daily fruit supply, some nice tropical fruits, put them in a bag, and gave them to me, insisting that I take what they had. No strings attached, no hands out for anything. The parting hugs were some of the sweetest I've ever known.

Most of us, not just Americans, are pretty limited in our exposure to and understanding of other people. That we might think differently, or that we might have different takes on values, ethics, and morals, doesn't mean that there still aren't overriding universal experiences, joys and pleasures. We can meet on common ground. In fact, we *must* meet on common ground.

Think for a moment about what that means about our traveling. Even though we give intellectual recognition to the fact that most other countries—even Western European countries—don't live the way we do, as travelers, we seem to forget what we know. Have you ever noticed how we come home after a travel vacation and we will recount having walked for a mile or having sweated for an afternoon, with the same sense of sacrifice and toil as if we had crossed the Rocky Mountains in a covered wagon?

I would say that the image that is projected of Americans in the popular, controversial book *The Ugly American* isn't so true. It seems to me that most Americans are generally kind (or want to be kind) and even generous, sometimes foolish because of the way we spend our money like water. Perhaps.

It seems that because of our relative physical isolation as a nation, and because we really only speak one language (again, because of our relative isolation), that we are actually quite culturally insensitive. I don't mean to sound mean or condemning; it's simply that we really aren't very international in our approach to life.

There is also this: in the last thirty or forty years there has really been significant immigration into the United States, particularly by Asians and Hispanics. That hasn't really sat all that well with us, and so our thinking about foreigners is not only from a point of isolationism, but also from perceived bad experiences with foreigners. We tend to carry that with us when we travel.

We really do expect the kinds of conveniences that we have at home, though in *conversation* we pretend to understand that for the most part, we won't be able to have them. We also tend to look down upon those peoples and cultures who don't have what we have, and we consider them less civilized in some respects. We don't like the look of poverty; we don't like seeing more occupants in a vehicle than is deemed permissible by the U.S. National Transportation Safety Board (like four adults on a moped, carrying two-by-fours); we don't like litter; we don't like different odors; we don't like harsh toilet paper; we get irritated when they don't speak English very well (it's usually *not* whether they speak it, but rather whether they speak it *well*).

Let's talk about a few examples. Values, ethics, and morals seem to be the overall categories where people make distinctions; in fact, because of those distinctions (differences), nations and national borders are established, religions are established, and within those religions denominations arise, all because of differences.

Most of the examples that I will offer relate to the Latin American countries. I could also give similar examples from Asian, African, or Middle Eastern cultures. For the most part, the values, ethics, and morals of Americans kind of blend with those of the Western Europeans—enough, at least, so that during travels or temporary visits, we can keep our relationships "on the surface," and whatever differences there are will have minimal impact on us.

The first example that leapt to my mind is the way we Americans distinguish between giving a tip and giving a bribe. Here is what the *American College Dictionary* says about the definition of a bribe (there are five meanings, but these two apply to our conversation):

1. money or any other valuable consideration given or promised with a view to corrupting the behavior of a

person, esp. in that person's performance as an athlete, public official, etc.

2. anything given or serving to persuade or induce

In our culture, in its purest application, don't we think about bribes as relating to public officials or athletes, those two main categories of profession? We don't like the idea of favoritism; we don't like the idea of competition being bridled or stifled in some artificial way. In American culture and in Latin American cultures, everyone is comfortable with tipping individuals who work in the service industry: waiters, waitresses, taxi drivers, porters, etc.

Now we come to institutional service. Let's say that during an investigation, we have discovered a big operation or some illegal industry that is located in a rural part of a Latin American country. In order to properly and legally investigate and to enforce the law, police, prosecutors, and judges must be involved. It is frequently the case that the rural judicial system simply does not have the supporting legal structure or infrastructure to provide the personnel (police, prosecutors, judges). So we would look for the closest geopolitical entity (the next larger entity that has jurisdiction), and we would ask them to participate.

Much of the time *they* don't have the necessary budget required to support that activity in an area that may be several hundred miles away. To be plain about it, the police, prosecutors, and perhaps a judge may have to travel several hundred miles and establish temporary quarters for a period of several weeks in order to participate in the prosecution of that illegal industry. Their agencies can't afford it. Period. No discussion.

So what do we do? The answer, in every one of those communities where budget is an issue, is *for the interested parties to pay for those expenses.* Again, wanting to be very plain, if a wealthy corporation (not necessarily an American corporation) wants to shut down an illegal industry that is illegally producing its product, the corporation frequently will have to pay the cost of the salaries, transportation and temporary housing for those public officials.

In the United States, that might be considered bribery. I say "might" because it does seem that these days, there is an increased willingness for public institutions to receive endowments or even grants from private sources. I know personally of several American corporations that refused to pursue the prosecution of known criminal entities that were significantly impacting the legitimate business of those corporations, and the reason was because the corporate officials believed that paying public officials was bribery. Of *course* there are abuses. I've just never personally seen any. Paying the government, directly, for personnel time never produced any particular result.

Some of you readers may agree with that. My point isn't to settle or smooth out the differences in these ethics and values and morals but rather to point out that the differences *exist* and that it would be well worth our time to gets "outside of ourselves" and consider the other system. I think you'll come to understand that at least some of the differences are quite arbitrary and really don't affect our own fundamental system of beliefs (religious beliefs, for example).

Just writing the words "religious beliefs" causes me to remember that the denominations within the Christian faith were established based on something as "important" as whether one sprinkles or dunks for a baptism. Of course there is more to the establishment of a separate denomination than just how one should baptize, but that singular distinction very well characterizes the basic argument. Today, most of us can kind of giggle about that. But it wasn't so many years ago when that little distinction was the basis of heated debate.

The last point that I want to touch on relates to thinking about money. Once again I'm making some gross generalizations, and at the risk of over-generalizing, I'll proceed. Americans don't know what a scarcity of money is, and I'm making that a specific statement as relates to the traveling American.

After all, an American who is traveling *has* money, doesn't he? Whether it is his own or his employer's doesn't matter. In fact, there are many countries in the world whose citizens are as wealthy as Americans. In one of the Latin American countries where I've done work, I learned that the police lieutenant who led the squad of men who helped us conduct a raid earned the equivalent of US $250 per month. He was very pleased to be making that amount of money. He and his men proudly took our group to their shooting range and allowed us to shoot their personal sidearms, and their rifles and semiautomatic weapons.

We were having an enjoyable time. Many of us had considerable firearms experience, and it was a real point of contact with these good men who were helping us. During a casual conversation with one of the men, somehow I happened to ask how they obtained their ammunition. He said, "Oh, we buy it with our own money." I asked if the ammunition was supplied by the agency for which they worked, and he replied that they were given one box of ammunition a year, with which they were expected to qualify at the range. I spoke to the men who were in our party; we figured out how many boxes of ammunition we had shot through, and we purchased that amount, and a little more, to give to our friends. (I don't even want to describe the poor condition of their shooting range. Their meager circumstances are sobering.)

In many foreign countries, just a small amount of money is often a point of literal survival. There are very few countries outside of Western Europe that have as many entitlement programs as do the United States. It can't be denied that the reason for some of the immigration to our country is based on the fact that there is governmental support available to immigrants. Once again, without getting into that discussion, the welfare systems that exist in most Latin American countries would not be considered sufficient for survival. That's easy to forget. For us, the poor are taken care of.

So what's my point with all of this? I'm not saying that we should throw away or even necessarily compromise our values, ethics, and morals. There remain certain things that are universally wrong. Let's keep those always in mind. Those things that are considered universally wrong are known in law as *malum in se*, or "wrong in and of themselves." There is another category of wrong, called *malum prohibitum*, which means "wrong because prohibited" or wrong because a law has been made about it. This is a standard definition (SEE Law.com:

> *Malum prohibitum* (plural *mala prohibita*, literal translation: "wrong because prohibited") is a Latin phrase used in law to refer to crimes made so by statute, as opposed to crimes based on English common law and obvious violations of society's standards, which are defined as *malum in se*. An offense that is *malum prohibitum*, for example, may not appear on the face to directly violate moral standards; an example is the law against insider trading, where the simple act of sharing information may not be wrong in itself, but only because of its context in a larger framework of regulated trading. Parking violations, speeding, driving

or fishing without a license, and voyeurism also fall in this category. There is a controversy whether copyright infringement is *malum prohibitum* or *malum in se*.

We will tend to combine or even confuse the distinction between those two. Let's stay true to our own distinctions and at the same time, think about and give consideration to those with others.

Tips

Without necessarily having to change anything (or much) of what you think and do, consider some of what we've been discussing, and be open to seeing and understanding that other people may see things differently. Different isn't necessarily bad. Ask yourself if your objection or discomfort about some thing or another is because you've always done it your way, or because you have never thought about doing it differently, or … just because. Remember, the Wright brothers may have been first to fly (and apparently that's debatable), but there were several others in different parts of the world who also flew within days of the Wright brothers. Here's another thought. Just because "they" do it differently doesn't mean you have to. You can very easily order a McDonald's in most foreign lands now, and it will almost taste the same. You won't *have* to eat the local cuisine. But you'll be missing something wonderful if you don't try.

Consider a different way. It'll change your perspective about travel.

Chapter 6
Contingencies
(or: What do we do if we get separated or stranded?)

This section is useful even if you *don't* travel! All families—any intimate, working, or fellowship group—should have certain emergency contingency plans in place. Work those out for you own family.

Have you ever gone anywhere with a group of vehicles in kind of a caravan situation? I think I must do that a couple of times a year. Have you ever led a group of vehicles from one place to another, particularly a long distance, for a number of hours on the road? I'll bet that at least once, one of the members of the caravan slowed down, or turned off, or in some way or another got separated or lost. Right? Have you had that happen?

If you were more clever than I (especially before cell phones), you might have prearranged a meeting spot or a phone number to call in such an event. Or maybe everyone independently knew where you'd be stopping next, or where you'd be stopping for the night. That would've made for a delightful outcome, wouldn't it? I'll bet, though, that at least most of you reading this hadn't done that kind of planning. When it happened, you said to yourself, "I wish we'd made some arrangement." You resolved to plan next time ... but didn't.

Think about it for today.

Even with cell phones, you go out with people for an evening. You get separated or someone gets sidetracked ... *and you don't know their cell phone numbers*. I know I, for one, have done that many times. It was months before I had my kids' cell phone numbers memorized. (Moms are way better about that.)

My wife and I made a cross-country move. I drove the moving truck, and she drove the car. Just two vehicles. Sounds easy enough, right? Wrong! Driving on the interstate at interstate speeds, if your mind wanders at all, the next thing you know, the other person's vehicle is out of sight. I don't even remember what state we were in when it happened to us. We were using two-way radios, but as it turned out, we were out of range. Right away, we both figured we had to be more than a mile or two apart. We had not established a "friendly number" that each of us could call; we hadn't even particularly discussed where we'd be stopping either for lunch or for the evening, for that matter. It probably wasn't more than half an hour before we found each other, one sitting on the side of the road near an off-ramp.

Here's part of the point:

1. Whenever it's practicable, all adults should know the same information about certain fixed events, such as when and where the next pit stop will be, or the next meal. Oh, also

where and when you'll land that evening. You can discuss that on virtually every trip, local or international.

2. Even if everyone has cell phones, every person of age (meaning anyone who can think and dial a phone) should also have at least one name and phone number of a person who can be called and be a point of contact. There may be more than one person, but there should be at least one.

3. There should be an agreed-upon rendezvous point in the event of separation. (I'll discuss this further.)

We were in a Latin American country, and we had completed an investigation regarding the importation of counterfeit electronic products. We had used sensitive information from informants and surveillance details, and the prosecutor agreed that it was time to present our case to the judge. We worked with the prosecutor a number of times in the past, and she was very trustworthy.

Because there is a high degree of illegal activity in the area, and because there are sporadic instances of judicial corruption, the system is such that when a case is to be brought before a judge, no one knows which judge it will be. That can be a good thing ... unless you get one of the questionable judges, right? At the time, there were five sitting judges, and they were selected by rotation. For the most part, as far as minimizing the corruption related to the judge, that system worked pretty well.

When the system failed, it usually was at the clerical level. In other words, we didn't find the prosecutors to be corrupt. The prosecutor would meet with us and double-check factual information that was being presented to the judge. The prosecutor would then go to the courthouse to find out which judge would be sitting on the case, and within an hour or two, he would be presenting the case to the judge. There was almost never any rejection of the case by the judge, and so he would sign the order and hand the order to a clerk.

This is where the potential problem began. We learned after our first or second raid that on one of those occasions, one of the clerks (we never learned which) got in contact with the bad guys and warned them. When we got to the raid location, the crew that was going to cover the rear of the buildings was just rounding the corner of the building to take up its position when they saw part of the group of the suspects throwing contraband out of a second-story window.

So we established a precise routine. Once the prosecutor presented the matter to the judge and he approved, even as he was handing the signed authorization, order, and search warrant to the clerk, the prosecutor called one of us by cell phone (for many Latins, the cell phone is the primary phone). This person was waiting with the federal policemen (depending on the size of the case, between ten and fifteen individuals), and she would let us know that the order had been signed. Our team member would then call the others, who would be waiting in another location. We would all drive quickly to the area where the raids would take place, in a couple of autos, a van, and two or three pickup trucks with uniformed, armed *federales*.

Even though cell phone service in that poor Latin country was better than that in the United States, on the day of one particular raid, the mountainous terrain or weather—who knows what?— prohibited our two crews from communicating. Happily, we had agreed that our point of contact in such an event would be a friend in the U.S. embassy, so each crew quickly contacted that person, and the day was saved.

So there we were two crews with about ten members each, no more than five to seven miles apart, yet we were communicating via an intermediary who was over two hundred miles away. It worked great; but if we hadn't established ahead of time that point of communication, the whole venture would have failed.

So let's talk about establishing some contingency plans. These are only guidelines, and each situation is going to offer different options. The point is, plan ahead, and have some points of contact (a variety of them) for *everyone* in your group to be able to use.

1. There should be a general, fail-safe point of contact; it can be a person, a family, or a business. That individual or entity will be known to every member of the party. If children are in your party, that information can be written down and stored someplace that will always be available to them. For small children, some people like to make a dog-tag-type necklace or use a bracelet with the ability to insert a small piece of paper; if they're older, they can put the paper in a wallet or pocket. For years, my elderly mother was virtually always at home, and if not, she was never away from her phone for more than an hour. She happily volunteered to be a point of contact.

2. After establishing that point of contact, there should be other points of contact for your travel along the way.

    a) If you're driving in tandem or in a caravan, that point of contact might be the person or entity at your destination.

    b) Once at your destination, you may have plans for travel, sightseeing, or business during the course of a day. Most of the time, if you're away, you'll be staying at a hotel, so a point of contact can be a hotel operator or the front desk.

3. Let's say you're in a foreign country, no one speaks the language, and not everyone has a cell phone. When you first arrive (perhaps even at the airport, where you'll almost always find an English speaker), you can easily find certain landmarks such as a famous-name hotel or a well-placed, easily located police department. Everyone should know that if members of the group get separated for any reason, you will all meet at the Holiday Inn (or you name it) and wait there until making contact with the rest of the party.

In fact, in probably almost every country, there are American-named establishments that are easy to identify and easy to remember, for adults and children. It's amazing—even a little embarrassing—how many places have a twenty-four-hour McDonald's. Sometimes they are not in the greatest neighborhoods, so one should know that kind of information. But you get the point.

An American embassy is not a bad point of contact, nor have I found it to be necessarily the best. They do have hours of business, and sometimes individuals who man the phones during the off hours might not speak English as well as the person at the McDonald's. Believe me, you don't need a very large piece of paper to write quite a lot of information that can be very helpful in the event of becoming separated or needing places to meet at a later time. Take along some three-by-five index cards (you don't need many); they're sturdy paper for this work.

I believe it's virtually imperative that at least one member of the party have a global cell phone. They are not expensive anymore. I use one company that offers both a $49 and a $99 cell phone that you purchase and own, and to which is permanently assigned an international phone number that you always keep. You pay for each individual call. You may never even use it.

The company I use happens to be based in the United Kingdom, and certain calls within that country are free. The calls are per minute and generally range someplace between a dollar and $2.50 a minute. Obviously this phone is meant for serious calling for emergencies only. The telephones are quality name-brand phones, the communication is very clear, and that's an extremely low price, particularly if you travel even just every few years. The difference between a $49 phone and $99 phone is basically that the $49 phone cannot be used for calls within the United States when in the United States. The $99 phone *can* be used within the United States when in the United States. (The $99 phone also includes a few more countries than does the $49 phone, but I haven't found that to be a significant difference.)

That kind of cell phone arrangement is, of course, just one option. Often you can rent a cell phone in the country you visit for someplace in the area of $50 for a couple of weeks. Another popular way of having an international cell phone, and one that you can use domestically, is by using a phone that has a SIM card slot. Popular phone service carriers such as AT&T, Verizon and T Mobile collectively describe SIM cards as does this concise Wikipedia description:

A Subscriber Identity Module (SIM) is a removable smart card available in two standard sizes, the first the size of a credit card (85.60 mm × 53.98 mm x 0.76 mm), while its more popular mini version has a width of 25 mm, a height of 15 mm, and a thickness of 0.76 mm. SIM cards store securely the key identifying a mobile phone service subscriber. The SIM card allows users to change phones easily by removing the SIM card and inserting it into another mobile phone, thereby eliminating the need for activation of the new mobile phone on the network. The use of SIM card is mandatory in the GSM world. The equivalent of a SIM in UMTS is called the Universal Subscriber Identity Module (USIM), whereas the Removable User Identity Module (RUIM) is more popular in the CDMA world.

Don't get too caught up in the technical part; just know that some phones have a card slot that allows communication from your phone to a particular telephone system. Some cards are called "international SIM cards." Those usually will enable the caller to communicate in, say, 140 different countries. Buying the card may cost in the area of $50. Local charges through that particular phone system will then be charged. There is almost always an expiration on the SIM card, usually a year or two. Sometimes the use of such a card can become a little tricky, and you may find yourself having to purchase individual SIM cards for different countries, depending on the country and phone system. But all in all, it's a viable solution.

Of our major cell phone carriers, I only know of one who seems to have produced a truly international phone that is able to recognize the several major, different kinds of cell phone systems. I won't get into the differences among those systems; it's pretty boring. But it can be important to know. It's information easily obtained.

It's useful for *every* member of the party to have enough money to be able to take a taxi to one of the agreed-upon meeting points. While it can be wonderfully useful to be able to say a few words in the native language, virtually every taxi driver will know what you mean when you get into the cab and simply say, "Marriott Hotel." Just remember, there may be a number of those hotels; if there are, you need to be able to identify which one. You might even consider getting a translation PDA.

You can receive a lot of help with this kind of thing at an airport or a car rental area. Even if you don't rent a car (which I don't particularly recommend), they will usually have a map of the area that you're visiting. Much of the time they will speak English, and you can look at the map and find potential meeting points. Or you can ask the desk attendant for that information, and you will be able to properly identify a specific hotel, for instance, either from the map or with the help of a clerk.

For example, in a Spanish-speaking country, you would identify one of the larger American chain hotels, and you might note that there are several in the area. You could arbitrarily choose the one that is in the center of town, and then either the map or the clerk would identify that as "Holiday Inn *en el centro*," or the Holiday Inn in the center of town. For a very timid or young person, write that instruction on a single piece of paper, and he can hand it to the taxi driver; the driver will take him there.

Depending on the age and maturity of the group, doing all of this might take between one and two hours of your time, before and during the trip. It's well worth the time, even for seasoned travelers. It is not something that even seasoned travelers do with any regularity. Also, especially with families, you don't want to do all of this planning and instruction with any sense of angst or fear. It's very easy to talk about and plan all of this and work up a good case of anxiety. That's not the point of this, is it? The point is to plan just enough to provide a good sense of security and safety, and to view such disruptions as a natural course of events, rather than as disasters.

If you think about it, you'll see that in the normal course of life, we actually do a lot of this sort of planning, and if there is a group and someone gets separated, if we keep our heads, we will all be able to think of that common place of meeting where we will all find each other. We're all headed for a common destination, right? If our family is headed for Grandma's, and if it's a day trip, that's the place we can all meet up. Of course, we should all know her address and/or phone number. If it's a trip several days long, it's easy enough to know that "on Monday night, we'll spend the night at the Holiday Express, exit 43 off Interstate 90 near Rochester." In almost every instance, if all the members of the party don't know that, at least several will. How much better if everyone knows!

Tips

1) Establish commonly known points of contact: telephone numbers and/or physical locations.
2) Give each member enough money to take a taxi to the agreed-upon point of reconnoitering.
3) For the young or timid (or weak-minded), provide a place of meeting or a common phone number on a sturdy piece of paper.
4) Know (or write down) a few words from the local language that will be helpful in the event of needing to meet someplace.
5) Give good consideration to having at least one member of the party be in possession of an international cell phone.

Chapter 7
Logistics of the Trip

Now this gets into more fun ... at least for me! I'm going to discuss a number of considerations that I'll include under the heading of logistics. This may be the chapter that almost everyone thought would be the centerpiece of the book. Maybe it is. These "let's get down to it" points of logistics are indeed important. In fact, unless you are a "*no le hace*" or "*on s'en fiche*" (meaning "who cares") person, I suppose any one of the points that we're going to discuss here could make or break the trip. So let's go over these points with an eye toward making it.

Flights: Times, Layovers (Advantages/Disadvantages)

This seems like a simple thing, doesn't it? After all, who doesn't know about flights and layovers? I don't want to make a simple thing difficult, but there are a few things to know and a few things to consider.

First, there are some international flights that pretty much fly *only* overnight or on what we could call a "red-eye" because if when it flies. Flights over long distances or through multiple time zones often fall into that category. It can be a good thing, because most of us can get some kind of sleep, and we can wake up at our destination and at least struggle through our first day there without losing, say, eight to twenty hours of our trip. Overnight flights also are not a bad thing if there are a number of small children on the plane. We can talk more about the actual flight under those circumstances later.

Second, when it comes to layovers, many of us have personal preferences about how long a time we want between flights. Usually there isn't too much practical concern about the transfer of luggage, so the consideration of layover times really becomes one of personal preference and the physical proximity of the gate at which you land, compared to the gate from which you take off on your next flight.

I'm going to get into the value of getting airport maps in a moment, but unless you fly pretty regularly, you may be surprised at how spread out airports can be these days. If you have rolling luggage or if you have small children, it can be twenty to thirty minutes of mildly brisk walking just to get from one gate to another. Some airports have moving sidewalks, and some airports have trams; that's something to find out. What you learn is that an airline usually has a section for its airplanes; the older, more established (or most influential, for whatever reason) airlines will have the more logistically appealing spots in the airport.

If you are connecting or laying over and are using the same airline, it usually means that your arrival gate will be relatively close to your departure gate ... *but not always.* You can ask your ticketing agent (if you use one) for gate information, and he may be able to give it to you in advance. With smaller airports, of course, this isn't too much of a consideration. I like at least thirty minutes between flights, preferably even more.

It's nice to know things like prevailing weather conditions. Do you know that in the United States, for instance, flying from the west to the east often means you'll pick up a nice tailwind, so that if you start a bit late, you can very often make up the time (and more) during that flight? The reverse can apply as well.

Of course, the airlines know that. But let's say you are flying from the East Coast to the West Coast and have to go through Chicago. Or you're flying from the United States to Latin America and have to go through Miami. Both of these airports are very busy. I find Chicago to have a kind of orderliness to the frantic pace. Miami? Just kind of nuts! I like a tad bit more time between my flights at these two airports. Both Atlanta and Chicago are quite spread out. JFK is a little better, but it seems like it's always under construction and everyone is bumping into each other. Again, I personally almost never have any problems with the transfer of luggage, no matter how close the flights.

I had been in the Atlanta airport several times before, and I really didn't have to pay much attention, as the flights were always on time or very close to one another. However, on my first trip to Central America, it was another story. I didn't know that the gates would be what seemed like miles apart. The flight arrived late, and I had approximately fifteen minutes until my connecting flight.

I usually walk fairly quickly anyway, and I rushed off the plane and checked with an agent directly inside. He told me that I had to travel to another concourse, and he directed me on my way. I like to think I pay attention, and that I read signs. But did I see any sign that directed me to a tram? No! I nearly ran for more than twenty minutes, and it was only when I was a few hundred yards from my new gate that I noticed a tram that would have gotten me there in two to three minutes. Hello! I really would've benefited from asking or from having studied an airport terminal map in advance. On that rare occasion, I missed my flight, but I ended up arriving in Central America only about two hours late.

And don't think that those "wild and crazy Latinos" have a monopoly on changing gates or concourses without any apparent reason. On a flight from New York to Salt Lake City, we changed gates four times, and we were moved as the weather conditions dictated the flight schedule and places of departure. Yes, some airports don't feel at all embarrassed to make the changes and never post the changes on their signs. However, they *do* make up for it by speaking rapidly and unintelligibly through their antiquated loudspeaker systems!

I have found it delightful to schedule some trips through the day intentionally. They may be harder to find than the overnight trips, but sometimes they're well worth it. It's worth spending a few minutes more to find out about what you'll be flying over, in order to make that decision. For instance, I mentioned that many or most flights from the United States to South America are red-eye flights. I don't know which trip it was when I finally realized that I had been flying over the Amazon region through the night hours and had never been able to see that wonderfully expansive jungle and river.

That discovery actually came to me when I was making a trip from the United States to South America via Santiago, Chile. I had a connecting flight through Chicago out of New York, and so I traveled from Chicago on a nonstop to Santiago. You'll probably recall from your geography days that the Andes stretch from north to south along the western part of South America.

On this particular trip, dawn was just breaking when our flight began to parallel the Andes from north to south; we were flying along the west side of those mountains, and the sun was rising over the peaks, many of which were snow-capped.

Similarly, when I flew from Santiago to Asunción, Paraguay, it was a day flight (only a few hours), and our flight route took us out of Santiago, initially paralleling the Andes on the west side, giving a fifteen- or twenty-minute aerial tour of the many open-pit copper mines in the area. Then it was over the mountains and on to Asunción. Wonderful! It was then that I realized that it might be worth giving up a half a day or a day by taking a daytime flight and seeing the wonders of the planet. (By the way, the Amazon from the air is breathtaking!)

There are many long-distance jaunts that are really worth taking a day flight and even sitting in a window seat. (And I'm a person who "has to" sit on the aisle.) Think ahead before finalizing your flights.

Get a Map of the Airport, Especially if Connecting

I've probably already made a good case encouraging you to get a map of the airport terminals through which you'll be traveling. I'll list a number of sites where you can get many of these maps very easily. Also, don't forget that many in-flight magazines have maps, though limited, of the terminals ... or some of the terminals. Today, with all of the cutbacks, who knows if airlines will continue producing their magazines? Not only that, but I find it comforting to have those maps at hand in advance so that I can plan my layover times, as mentioned above. They don't take up a lot of room, and you can put them in the back of one of your books. Look at the end of this chapter for some links to sites.

Hotels: Location as Well as Quality

So you can understand a little bit about my advice in this section, it might be helpful for you to know a couple of things about my preferences. I like nice hotels. If you have the opportunity to get to know an area, you may find that there isn't a great deal of difference between a three-star and a five-star except for the huge leap in price. Sometimes—many times—you'll find an *older* hotel that has some older luxury features and character (and no, I don't hide cockroaches, garbage, foul odors, or high crime rates under the euphemism "character"). And you might actually find that these older hotels are located in more convenient parts of town. In most foreign nations, the great rush to modernize (often to please Americans and Europeans) started a little later than it did in the United States. What that means is that often the old luxury hotels, along with many fine restaurants, operas, museums, and government buildings, are centrally located in the large cities and are some of the best hotel buys available for today's travel. Yes, there is an increasing tendency to tear down old buildings and erect new ones like we do, but in many instances the newer hotels are a bit less conveniently located.

Not only that, but I find that some of the older classy hotels are either family-owned or single-proprietor businesses, and they frequently emphasize excellent service. I have to say, however, that (as with the food) I have never encountered a bad hotel experience anywhere in Latin America. That certainly may not be the case for everyone, and indeed I'm prejudiced.

So if you've done any planning at all, if you've looked online for even the most superficial information about the city or cities to which you are going to travel, you'll be able to poke around the Internet a bit and find out the best locations for your hotels.

And from there, I'd suggest that you at least consider one of the older ones. Again, use good sense.

Look for photographs, and notice if the people in the photographs are wearing contemporary dress, or if automobiles are relatively contemporary (if you can identify the automobiles at all). I suppose everyone does this, but the Latins are not beyond posting older, better-looking photographs of their facilities in order to attract customers. I've gone into hotels and said to myself, "Ah, the photograph I looked at was taken in 1922." Again, I've never been disappointed, and those kinds of rare times have actually provided some good humor.

Passport and Visa

As of January 23, 2007, virtually all out-of-country travel will require a passport. Interestingly, pretty much all foreign nationals have had their passports "forever." We are just getting around to it. (We're still afraid of national identity cards!)

Not all of the travel pages of my current passport are stamped, but most of them are. There are a total of twenty-six pages in this, one of our most important documents. Since fifteen pages are dedicated to travel stamps, that means that there are eleven pages devoted to other things. Some of those pages are more important than others. The first seven pages have your photograph, personal information, and general declarations made by the State Department to the traveler. The last four pages are reserved for what they call "Amendments and Endorsements" … or explanations. You'll see some pictures of the passport later.

It is to the first pages that we should give our attention. These instructions aren't like reading instructions to put together a swing set, so don't ignore them! Some of this is important stuff, and this information not only is useful for us while we travel, but it also gives us insight into the attitude and policies of the United States government.

Some of this communicates things to other countries about what we (the government's voice) think about ourselves and what we think of other countries. Yes, other nationals know what our documents say, especially those important people who handle our passports: immigration, customs, hotel personnel, and some business personnel as we make purchases. It would be a great idea to know what these pages say. What should we know? How can others read them?

Starting on the third page, the U.S. government actually does a pretty nice job of providing advice for the traveler. Read and pay attention to this information.

At the end of the chapter, I will provide some links for you to use to learn about which countries require visas, the kinds of visas that are available in those countries, and the lengths of time that those visas might be valid.

Should you use a private passport service or not? You know what? For just a few extra dollars—that means $50 to $100—you can use a passport service to take care of your visa requirements or even to expedite your passport. These services are available through the Internet. I'll provide a few links for them as well; I found them to be quite reliable and

to save a great deal of time. These services are located in major cities where there are embassies nearby, where they can hand-carry your passport and get the visas for you. They can get it done for you as quickly as a few days or, at a relaxed pace, within two weeks. Getting it done in a few days requires a "rush" fee. I've used that method. It works.

As of this writing, the government cost for an adult passport is $97; for a service to obtain one, it's $157. For minors under sixteen years of age, it was $82; for a service, $142. *Visa fees are extra,* whether directly through the government or with a service, and they are $67 for renewal by mail.

According to the State Department, "The U.S. Electronic Passport (e-passport) is the same as a regular passport with the addition of a small contactless integrated circuit (computer chip) embedded in the back cover. The chip securely stores the same data visually displayed on the photo page of the passport, and additionally includes a digital photograph. The inclusion of the digital photograph enables biometric comparison, through the use of facial recognition technology, at international borders. The U.S.  e-passport also has a new look, incorporating additional anti-fraud and security features." It looks like these images from the U.S. State Department. The front's the same.

For information about visas, check the links I've provided on my website, www.SecretsForTravel.com. Just know that visas can range from a few dollars to as much as about $200. Their length of usefulness can vary a great deal. Some countries will issue a visa good for only one or two entries into that country; others will issue a visa for ninety days or six months with unlimited ingress and egress (entry/exit), and in some instances, you can get a visa valid for as long as five years.

For most visas, you have to provide some kind of explanation for why you are asking to come to their country. That is usually not a difficult or burdensome request. It may require a simple statement saying that you want to vacation there, or in the instance of business, you might need a letter from your employer confirming your need to travel and a phrase describing your purpose.

In all instances that I know, you need to list your points of contact within the country to which are traveling. That may be simply the hotel, or a friend's or relative's home. Most of the time you need a round-trip plane ticket (or other conveyance) as well. The foreign country likes to know that you have the ability to go home! Just so you don't feel too uncomfortable about that ...

again, depending on the country and the individual. (Yes, it can be quite political!)

Someone coming to the United States may have to provide a financial statement, proof of employment, and proof of earning a certain amount of income. He may be limited to a very short visit in the United States, even if he is the most attractive visitor. (Or he may choose to simply walk across one of our expansive, unguarded borders.)

Now, all of that said, may I give you an April 2007 update? My family and I are traveling to Europe in a few days. As of four days (including Easter weekend, to add to the pressure!) before the trip, we couldn't find my daughter's passport! Fun?

So I called several of the agencies I know who specialize in expediting passports and/or visas. They have a human take your paperwork and walk it over to the passport/visa place appropriate to your travel. You give them an authorization to act on your behalf. They'll promise twenty-four-hour service. *Question them carefully as to what that means!* The fastest turnaround I've ever had has been three workdays. It was well worth the approximate $200 in rush fees. We had no choice about traveling last minute; we *had* to get to our destination.

In the instance of my daughter, for this trip, the agencies couldn't perform. To make a long story short, I called our local congressman's office. Each member of Congress has someone who is assigned to work on just such matters: rush passports. In twenty minutes, this man called the closest passport-issuing office (that by experience, he knew would perform); in this instance, it was Boston. As it turns out, as a general rule, each of the issuing passport offices will take emergency requests. You have to show up in person. You have to show proof of the imminent travel—a ticket—and take along the other usual documentation: birth certificate, driver's license, statement of loss of passport, and two State Department application forms. So we were off to enjoy Boston and a fresh bowl of New England clam chowder while we got the new passport issued! It's nice to know that *anyone* can do that in an emergency.

Currency

There are three main things to remember about currency:

1) Please have at least a close, general idea about the exchange rate in whichever countries you are going to visit. It's very easy to get rates currently, and they will put you close enough that you won't have to feel embarrassed about getting a terrible rate when you buy something.
2) Except in the most anti-American countries (I've not encountered one personally), *everyone* takes U.S. dollars. Even in those countries where they are delighted that the American dollar may be weak at any given moment, they want our money. (Some merchants may grumble.)
3) Using plastic at every convenient opportunity is probably the best way to ensure getting at least a fair rate, if not the best.

With those considerations in mind, if you can *conveniently* get between $20 and $50 in local currency, it's nice to have that for unexpected taxi rides or for tip money. That said, service workers delight in receiving U.S. dollars ... generally. Part of the difficulty can be that we may not travel with the right denominations of U.S. dollars. Don't expect that the locals are going to have very much change! Do I need to repeat that? *Don't expect locals to have change for U.S. currency.*

If Americans can look ugly, dealing with currency is often the place where that look will appear. Here is the scenario: we may have had a long flight. We may even have experienced some stress in our layovers. For some reason, we are a little surprised when we get off the plane and everyone is speaking a foreign language. I've been there; I've thought those thoughts. "Why are all these people speaking Portuguese?" (Never mind that I've just landed in São Paulo.) I don't know why it happens. Maybe because after thirteen hours and a stiff neck, poor sleep, small bags of peanuts, and no pillows, I'm not on my game. I don't know.

So I found out that Brazilians don't really like to speak Spanish; I think I've survived an adventure because I've made it through immigration and customs (again, never mind that most personnel in the airport are multilingual and most signs are in English ... I'm still kind of proud that I've made it through these two obstacles).

Now, if I have plenty of luggage, I'll push my cart toward the curb, and the great rush begins from all of the young men who are willing to carry my bags. That throws me off a little bit. To be quite honest, I'm more used to the American porters or redcaps, who are, very frankly, kind of resentful and sometimes surly. In a foreign port, by contrast, twenty or thirty young, eager faces rush my way, hoping they'll get my business. I get kind of caught up in that; it's kind of nice to see eagerness in such a humble position, and you know that they're not part of a union, they're not getting benefits, and they may not even be there tomorrow.

Upon even a little reflection, you also know that they may be significant breadwinners in their families. So my heart warms a bit, and I decide that I might share my wealth. I know I've looked with no small amount of humor upon a nine-year-old boy trying to lug my sixty-pound bag and doing quite a manly job of it! However, I had two more bags! So his former competitor becomes his partner, and they work quite smoothly together. They might guide me out to their brother or cousin or other relative, who is a taxi driver.

I've always gotten out to the curb, I've always had help getting a taxi, and I've never lost a thing. So there I stand, and these two eager boys are ready to put the bags in the taxi or on the hood, or wherever I indicate. The taxi driver might bark at them; sometimes the boys even retreat fifteen or twenty feet. Now "the currency problem" might arise. Dang it!

I reach into my pocket, and as I do so, those faces light up like it's Christmas morning. So I'm feeling pretty good. But in my hand, all I have is a twenty. Now comes the dilemma.

Do you get the point?

I've probably covered that one with every option that you can think of. I've asked for change from the taxi driver, the nearby adult porter, the young lads themselves; I've gone to a rental agency or a tourist booth in an attempt to either get change for the U.S. currency or to quickly make an exchange for the local money. When I've been able to make the currency exchange, it's usually been at a sacrificial rate.

Here's another thing you don't want to do (and yes, I probably do it at least once per trip): don't pull your hand out of your pocket with a handful of local currency and stick it out toward the vendor, expecting them to take the proper change. That's really, really, really easy to do. There is even a strange sense of satisfaction in doing that. "Look at me! I can be foolish ! I can *afford* to lose money!" So if you're buying something on the street from a person who is obviously a local, at least try to control the loss some. If you've paid any attention at all to the exchange rate, you know what the equivalent of US$10 or US$100 is. That's an easy conversion, usually. Guesstimate the maximum price of the thing you're buying, and use your "tens" arithmetic to limit how much is in your hand.

If you know the local currency and you are still generous, you'll gain a surprising respect. It's kind of funny, if you think about it. These American tourists obviously have enough money to be traveling, right? Usually if you have money, it means that you've achieved a modicum of success, right? And when it comes to currency exchange, we act as dumb as bricks! How could we possibly have earned the money to take this trip in the first place?

I do have to say that for the most part, Americans are fairly generous. Sadly, the percentage of those who are "out to rape and pillage" is large enough that it colors most people's feelings about us. On the other hand—and I won't go into any detail—there are some emerging nations whose people act like they're still living in the Depression, so their view of any prosperous nation is often flavored by bitterness and resentment, all the while *yearning* for American dollars, even today.

So don't be surprised about the currency thing and react negatively. There will come a time when you have to dig in your pocket and spend some cash. Consider that in advance. Just like we'll talk about the six or eight opportunities to give tip money from the time you leave home until you arrive at your hotel, we will also emphasize the need to be able to respond in these currency "crises."

Luggage

Boy, luggage! What a wide variety of choices! Acknowledging that there are many ways to go, I'm going to give you my own particular preferences when it comes to luggage. I'll also give you my reasoning, and you can take it or leave it.

By far, I prefer soft-sided luggage with a rigid or semirigid frame. You can actually do pretty well for not very much money. In every instance that it's practicable, I like for every piece to be able to roll. Pay attention to the rollers! You can buy fairly inexpensive luggage with very adequate rollers. I don't like the little ball-type rollers; I like the roller-skate type.

I take a carry-on bag, usually a computer-type case that will fit under the seat. No matter what all of the "authorities" advertise, there is a considerable variation in the space beneath the seats and in the overhead compartment. You need to get a feel for that. I've mostly been successful with a standard-sized computer case with rollers, no deeper than about nine inches; I've found that most seats have that kind of space underneath. We will talk more about connecting flights, but be aware of the fact that on some short commuter flights, the aircraft may take almost no under-seat luggage. That means that you'll have to hand it to a flight attendant as you're boarding the plane, and they'll put it in the belly. I alert you to that fact because many of us take computers or cameras or other electronic equipment, and you may be faced with having to release that to someone who could throw it underneath. Melancholy.

I have a couple of rigid-side suitcases. There's no particular need to discuss the size. *Always be sure you have wheels on this bag, even if you're not going to be carrying it yourself.* I don't carry hanging bags anymore. I haven't found them to deliver hanging clothing in any better shape than if I'd packed them carefully in a suitcase. Yes, there are some expensive hanging bags that will do a better job. But I don't want to spend the bucks! A little-known secret is that in most foreign cities, not only will they have irons in the rooms, but also their laundry service is usually very, very reasonable. More on that below.

Let's talk for a moment about securing and identifying your bag. Because of the way security is these days, it's a little difficult to totally lock your bag. Some security areas will allow you to lock it after they've conducted their inspection, but most won't. Those that will allow you to even come near your bag after the inspection would also allow you to put a lock on it, no doubt. From a practical standpoint, I've done a couple things.

For just a few dollars, you can get a quick-releasing nylon web strap that has a unique color to it, and wrap it around the outside. This will make it less likely that your bag will open during transit, and it will make your bag a little bit more identifiable as it's making its way around the baggage carousel. I also like individual, brightly colored identification tags. Some of those fluorescent-colored happy-face tags work just fine. In fact, if a thief sees it, he may think it belongs to a child and ignore it !

Whatever you use, you'll want to eliminate or greatly reduce anything hanging loosely or sticking out much from your bag. Those kinds of objects can get stuck in the baggage handling mechanisms or stuck to another bag.

I'll discuss this in the next chapter, but I like to avoid putting anything in my check- through luggage that's not fairly easily replaceable. If I can carry important electronic items, I do so. I also try to take a couple of important clothing items in my carry-on bag, maybe a toothbrush, a stick of deodorant, and a safety razor, just in case ... but don't go nuts! All of a sudden, your carry-on bag can become one of those items that everybody moans about when they see you walking down the aisle inside the plane. You know, the guy with two hand-carry-sized bags, pulled along on wheels, ones he'll never be able to put under the seat or overhead!

Plastic Seal Bags for Packing

In the last two or three years, I have discovered the technique of packing clothing in plastic bags. For $10–$20 you can buy six or eight commercially made bags that are a little heavier than large freezer bags but not particularly better. I have bought them, and I'm glad, because they're very useful. It really is true that if you fold clothing carefully, put it in a bag (even a paper bag), and roll it up, it arrives in very good condition, for the most part.

You really don't even need the bags for the items to arrive in good shape, but the difficulty comes at the baggage checks in security. I'm sad to report that this is truer in American terminals than in most foreign terminals: some baggage-checking security personnel seem to have some kind of personal contest going to see how upside down they can turn the contents of your bags while they do their checking. And of course, you can't say anything, for fear of getting shot.

In those instances when you can watch the baggage inspection take place, it's quite satisfying to see them look in your items and shuffle them around a bit in the enclosure bag, leaving everything pretty much in good shape. The first time I saw that, I felt like I had won a one-on-one basketball game with someone.

Shrink-Wrap

Did you know that now you can shrink-wrap luggage—wrapping items in plastic wrap, usually with a large machine? I think this has fascinating possibilities; however, I have to admit having had little direct experience with it. I've never used the service. But I've been with people who have used the service, and I've seen it many times. Not all airports have shrink-wrapping facilities, and as with everything, there are pluses and minuses.

In the plus category, your bag will be inspected and then completely shrink-wrapped, making it pretty water-resistant. That gives the bag itself some protection against scuffing; it virtually ensures that it won't come open even under relatively harsh handling, and it significantly reduces the temptation to tamper with it. Right now, wrapping your luggage also makes it somewhat more distinctive than other bags, since the clear majority of them are not wrapped. Add a bright tag underneath the wrapping, and you'll have a unique and easily identifiable bag.

On the minus side, there is the possibility of random inspections, which would mean that the wrapping would be removed. Or you might have multiple connections where your luggage might not be checked through. In other words, you might end up paying for the wrapping for just a part of your trip. I suppose one could also make the argument that by wrapping the bag, you might be bringing attention to it. I don't know; I don't think so.

The cost isn't terribly high; as of this writing, it ranges someplace between $5 and $10 per bag. You'll need to plan on taking just a little extra time … at least a few minutes. I've seen this to be very popular in South American countries. Look under Tips (Page 102) for a couple of Web references.

What to Be Sure to Take

Your must-have items list will vary considerably depending on where you're going. My list is a lot shorter if I'm not going to one of the poorer countries. (The politically correct term might be "emerging nations" or, as a last resort, "Developing nations.") However, there'll be many items that you want to take wherever you will be traveling.

You can buy a one-pint **water bottle and filter** for maybe $15 from any one of a variety of websites, such as Cabelas (www.cabelas.com), and the filter will be sufficient to cleanse your water well enough to pass pretty much all of the common bacterial tests (and certainly the big chunks … yuck, did I say that?). That's not a bad idea. It doesn't take up a lot of space. If you find yourself in a questionable area, fill the darn thing up with the best water you can find, and then you simply drink through a straw, which is connected to the filter. So there's not a long wait for the water to purify. (Don't forget, if you are in an obvious "bad water" area, you'll want to brush your teeth with purified water, and you'll want to avoid ice cubes.)

Consider a thin **digital camera** and memory cards. How much of a picture taker are you? You may want to take a digital camcorder, or you may be satisfied with a decent point-and-shoot digital camera that also has some humble video capabilities. Those can be very small, and you can buy a nice-quality one that will go in your shirt pocket. Or take a bigger camera, if you want to tote it around and want greater photographic capability. If you want to spend a few bucks, they even have high-quality digital camcorders that fit in the palm of your hand and also take high-resolution still photographs. That's a whole other subject, and the only thing that I will mention here is that if you choose a nice, small digital camera that is primarily used for still photos, you'll either want to have multiple memory cards or be able to transfer the photos in some fashion. There is a variety of choices, but here's food for thought: a nice, major-brand, compact, high-resolution camera can fit in your shirt pocket or purse—all but disappear—and yet be available to record your trip.

Bring at least one universal **plug adapter** (page 162) for electrical appliances. If you're taking any kind of equipment along with you, don't forget that most foreign countries have either different electrical plug fittings or different power ratings … often both. If you're taking along a laptop, the power adapter that you'll be taking virtually always accommodates any power rating differences. What you do need to be able to do is make your plug fit.

There are inexpensive plug kits available through most of the chains—Wal-Mart, Target, Kmart, etc—that will allow you to plug your accessory into a local electrical outlet. That will be true for each electronic product you have with a U.S. electrical power plug fitting. You can also buy such an adapter when you get to the country to which you are traveling.

This can sometimes be a little tricky, because you'll need to find out where they're being sold and then get to that location. Sometimes a hotel gift shop or a store might carry them. Don't depend on it. You might want to print out the chart that I've added to the Tips at the end of this chapter so that you will know which plug endings you'll need. For each electrical item that doesn't have a power adapter (that's most), you'll need to look at the individual product and see what the power range or reading is for the product. What I have found is that many products will accommodate the different power systems in different countries, and all that is needed is the plug adapter to be able to plug it in.

What about a **phone card**? This is an area where there are a ton of options. Some people don't want to be bothered at all with a phone on their trip. That's part of why they are "going away." Cool.

I personally like to have a phone, and perhaps only to use it in the rare instance when it is an emergency. (What that really means is when it might be important to get directions or speak to a host or business associate to inform him of a meaningful schedule change.) I'm aware of one U.S. phone service as of this writing, Cingular/ATT, that has a true international phone. I have used one, and it was … okay. I have purchased an international phone with a dedicated phone number that I always keep. I have no subscription fees, and I pay per call. The rates are similar to regular phones, and sometimes they're cheaper.

Another option is to have a phone credit card with pre-purchased minutes or minutes that you can easily purchase from where you are. (By the way, in most foreign countries, most operators speak English. That means you can purchase minutes for your phone credit card pretty easily.) The only minor difficulty is that in using such a phone card, you may have to go through an operator.

These suggestions for logistics and planning are very general and not meant to be totally inclusive. Your individual activities and individual needs will no doubt bring in other things to consider. My desire here is simply to draw your attention to the fact that planning can make a big difference to the success of your trip.

Tips

Shrink wrap information besides page 158:
http://www.pprune.org/passengers-slf-self-loadingfreight/354111
-shrink-wrapping-luggage.html

and

http://www.worldbaggage.com.au/cgibin/gen.cgi?action=genpag
e&pageid=secure_wrap

See Resource Pages beginning page 157 for specific links and websites related to the following:

- Passport information
- Currency conversion

- Airport terminal maps
- Luggage and shrink-wrapping
- Cell phones/country codes
- Electronic products and electric outlet adapters (pictures, charts)
- Voltage regulators

Chapter 8
The Actual Travel

Can it be? *Now* we're going to talk about the travel? Yes, indeed!

Attitude

Let me mention this again. First, we talked a little bit about the attitude we have toward people in general, and now I'm going to discuss it briefly in terms of the travel itself. Please set aside any thoughts like, "I like *being* at my travel destination, but I *hate* getting there," or anything even sounding like that. If you moan, groan, and complain; if you set yourself up (which is exactly what it is) by thinking negatively about the actual travel, then you will experience exactly what you've been thinking. Oh, sure, all of us have gotten someplace on a trip and said, "That went a lot better than I expected." That's not what I'm talking about. (In fact, I'd say that if you had a better experience than you expected, your positive attitude almost certainly had something to do with that result.)

The actual travel can be a lot of fun. You're going to be sitting next to people that you've never met before, and one of the bonuses is that you may never see those people ever again. Now, I say that's a bonus not because you don't want to ever see them again, but rather because knowing it's unlikely you'll ever see them again, you can relax, look forward to meeting and talking to a complete stranger, and hearing about new things and new lives.

What to Wear for Travel and Why

This section isn't about getting clever hints about how to wear the best thing for every weather condition, but I believe there are still some things to keep in mind. Just *think* about what you might wear. Once again, these are very personal comments, and everyone can certainly wear whatever they choose. Some people still "dress" when they fly. I do too, but it's dressing for comfort and ease. What do I mean?

First, remember, you're not going to be walking to the airport or to the docks or to wherever your departure point is. You'll likely be driving. That's going to be true upon arrival as well. We sometimes dress as if we're going to actually be outside, in the elements, whether hot, cold, rainy, or snowy. I live in a very snowy climate. During the winter, some people dress for the day *as if they're going to be playing in the snow* rather than being out in the weather only as long as it takes to walk from their heated automobile to their heated office space, store, or whatever. That's always perplexed me. So dress down, and carry a heavy coat in the trunk in case you get stranded and have to walk outside! I only fleetingly consider the weather on either end.

If it's going to be quite cold, I only bring along a light jacket and wear a long-sleeved shirt on board. So for the *travel* portion,

I see no need to specifically dress for weather. Once you're there, it's a different matter. If I'm presenting at a conference, I'll not be outside much. If we're doing raids, we'll be outside, so take clothes accordingly.

Second, the most important part of dressing for the actual travel is really about passing through security. Life is way, way easier if you can breeze through security. At least half of "breezing through" revolves around what you're wearing. Let's start from the bottom and work our way up.

I'd say that at least half the time, you have to remove your shoes. Wear some shoes that you can slip on and off with ease, preferably without laces. And even with those, as much as is practicable, wear shoes that have no steel shanks in the arches, etc.

I've been in the habit of wearing cargo-style pants, many times with zip-off legs. Those silly zippers can be a real security line stopper. So I get pulled out of line, and they go over me with the hand wand. Sometimes they have to do it two or three times just to figure out that it's the zippers causing their alarm. Sometimes trousers with heavy zippers, large metal buttons, or other metal appendages are going to slow down the process. Once they pull you out of line, smooth passage through security can be kissed goodbye.

Then there is the belt. I pretty much automatically pull mine off and put it into one of the trays, letting it go through the machine on the hand-carry belt. Many times they are asking passengers to remove a sweater or a jacket and put it in one of the plastic tubs.

Here's what I do with anything metal in my pockets or on my wrists, including cell phone, etc. I put all of that, along with my watch, in a pocket of my carry-on bag; and of course, I put that bag in one of the plastic tubs. Carry along a small, Ziplock-type baggie. This is especially good for loose change! I usually carry ten to fifteen coins; they are a pain to deal with when unloading your pants pockets and reloading them. If I do all of what I've mentioned, security is a breeze.

We are currently traveling in days when most airlines have removed their pillows and their blankets—so indeed, you may need a sweater for your flight.

Luggage

Here might be a good place to discuss the current baggage situation. Supposedly, because of increased fuel costs, flying weight considerations have resulted in some airlines (soon all) to be charging for *all checked* bags. They continue with their policy of allowing one carry-on bag and a hand-carried item. Some trips demand that we take along enough stuff to have to check a bag. How about light travel?

Well, here's some semi-good news. If you put a little thought into your carry-on bag, you can take along a pretty good amount of stuff. I have a bag, for instance, with one hard plastic side and one soft side, making it flexible. It is narrow, about seventeen inches wide (most are twenty inches or wider), and the important thing is that it's about six inches deep … depending. That fits in the overhead compartments of most airliners. Now, what I just said is something to consider: are you flying on a standard large aircraft? Some connecting flights utilize "commuter" style aircraft: that carry between twenty to seventy-five passengers. Both the overhead compartments and the areas under the seats are smaller. So find out!

But so far, there is no weight limit to the carry-on bag, which I find strange.

What to Take

Again, this is extremely subjective, isn't it? You are going to determine exactly what you want to carry, and my main objective here is simply to get you to think about it. No matter how orderly an airline, an airport, or a nation is in moving passengers, it always feels like there is a lot of pressure or even rushing when it's time to board your aircraft. Even after you've passed through security, even when you've juggled all of your carry-ons through that process, once you start boarding a plane, what you're carrying on really hits you.

Will I have to put it in the overhead? Do I actually have too many bags? Well, there is good news! Ladies, for some reason there seems to be a bias when it comes to carry-on bags. It seems that a purse is not counted as one of the carry-on bags. (Except maybe in Rome; see Chapter 11.) Flight personnel ignore backpacks, so I regularly see ladies with four, or even five, of what I would term to be carry-ons.

Lest the men feel left out, we can kind of make up for it by attaching certain items to our belts. The backpack trick works for us too!

Just think it through. What should you carry, and what shouldn't you? I don't think the decision is terribly difficult. As mentioned previously, I don't check anything that I think won't withstand rough handling. I *never* check my computer, period! If they deem that my laptop bag is too large to fit under the seat or in the overhead compartment (and many times, they're wrong), I've learned not to fight with them for fear of getting shot, so I take my laptop out of my case and carry it in my arms.

If I'm *really* not going to use the item, I put it in my checked bags. That goes for cameras, books, and other items that in my dream world, I think, "Oh, boy, now I have a chance to use this." The fact is, you can figure on ten to twenty minutes of time for both takeoff and landing, time in which doing anything meaningful is usually not going to be possible. Most of us are then occupied with the in-flight magazines, the sky traveler shopping magazine, and maybe one section of the newspaper that was left in the seat pocket in front of you. There's another hour gone. So approximately two hours are gone. Now what are we *really* going to do? At this point you'll fidget with your ticket, study your map of the terminal, figure out where you're going to land, and then play a couple of games of Pac-Man or hangman on your cell phone.

Consider: do you really want to tote that item around? Will you *really* use it?

Checking In

Mostly we're traveling with electronic tickets. If you've made your reservations well enough in advance, you've already selected your seats. Once you get to the airport, you can choose to go to one of the small ticket kiosks, or you can go to the ticket counter for assistance. In either case, your main activity at this point will be dealing with your luggage. Usually your luggage will be tagged, and you'll be sent on to luggage inspection. Much of the time, you can simply carry your bags over to the inspection station, where they will ask you if it's yours, and usually you can leave it and be on your way. Some airlines are checking your bags at the counter ... for you. No accompanying necessary.

Sometimes you will be asked to wait while the inspection is processed, and then you'll be sent on your way. If you have an idea about the layout of the airport, you'll also have some idea about how far the gates are from the ticketing and luggage inspection locations; you can gauge your time accordingly. Recently we were told that *after* passing through security, we'd need twenty minutes to get to the gate.

How much time should you allow in advance of takeoff? For domestic flights, it's recommended to be at the airport about ninety minutes in advance, a couple of hours for international flights. Do this if you can. But I think wisdom, mixed with a little bit of knowledge, can trim *some* time off of that, depending. If you know about your flight and it's not a big or completely full flight (you can be told that kind of information if you ask in advance), then you can be at the airport sixty to seventy-five minutes in advance—don't tell anybody I suggested that. Don't be fooled by early-morning flights; don't assume that they won't be busy. There are lots of early-morning flights that people use just like commuter flights. They are sometimes the most highly booked flights.

What to Anticipate

Anticipate a smooth flight and smooth processing. It makes such a difference in your attitude if you anticipate good things. I think you can anticipate encountering any number of airport workers who speak English as a second language. That is even more likely at some of the bigger airports like JFK, Dulles, Chicago/O'Hare, Dallas/Fort Worth, Miami ... not so much in LA. Don't worry about all of the challenges that come with the territory.

Anticipate needing to have your identification available several times. Get a document carrier/wallet that accommodates your passport, have it readily available, and life will be a lot smoother. You have to show your identification at the ticket

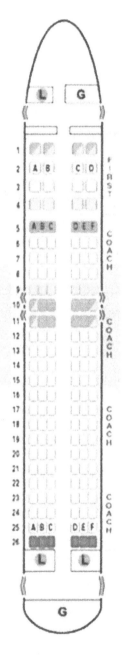

One airline even offers the above guide for passengers

counter and baggage inspection area; you'll have to show it at the security gate, along with your boarding pass; you may have to show it again when you board. Don't keep putting it back in your back pocket or in your big, old purse; have it available for each site.

Anticipate needing or wanting to go to the bathroom *before* you board. It's okay to talk about these things, is it not? You may be so caught up in getting a bag of peanuts or a candy bar that you forget to go to the bathroom. Don't! You may have to wait a long time to get into the bathroom on the aircraft, and who wants to use that one anyway?

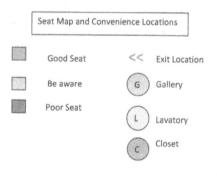

Anticipate the strong likelihood of having to wait over an hour at the gate, especially if you've arrived at the airport ninety to 120 minutes ahead of your flight.

What to Expect

It may seem like I'm being the master of the obvious, but the first thing you can expect is what you are bringing to the flight. If you anticipate goodness and joy, you'll be amazed by how many people that influences, from the flight attendants to the many people sitting around you (not just the person next to you in your seat).

You can expect relatively cramped flying conditions. Some airlines are definitely better than others in terms of seating. If you like a little legroom, once again, don't forget that the emergency rows and the bulkhead rows offer better legroom.

Though the partition isn't shown, the bulkhead would probably be in front of the seats ABCDEF. The bulkhead is a wall in front of the first seats of a section—plenty of legroom! Easy exiting from a window seat! (See Tips for a website with many airline seat configurations.)

Flying: Comfort Items for Travel

How long is your flight? And in what kind of plane are you flying? You have to know how long you can sit before you feel like you need or want to sleep. For me, during any flight of about four hours or less, I have zero desire to nap. Who knows what the temperature is going to be on board? I'm usually warmer than I am cool, so the most "over clothing" that I will take might be a sweatshirt or sweater. I almost never take a coat.

Again, depending on the airline, they will pressurize the interior cabin at somewhere around 5,000 to 6,000 feet of pressure (as if you were in the mountains at about 5,000 or 6,000 feet). So you might want some gum to chew, for your ears, as you ascend and descend. There is now a product, made by Cirrus, called EarPlanes, that is a specialized insert for the ear that "naturally regulates air pressure." I've not used them; I chew gum or just open my mouth a lot; but I've heard good reports about them. (No, I own no stock!)

I like those inflatable pillows, the kind that go around your neck. If I'm reading or (heaven forbid) I nod off, those funny donut-type inflatable rings keep your head from snapping or bobbing unceremoniously. Now, they *do* make you look awfully silly! But they work. I like items that increase comfort, but not at the expense of being fairly trim with carry-ons.

Because with the passage of time our breath gets rather stale, I like to have a piece of gum or a breath mint for when I arrive, or in case I actually decide to speak to someone sitting next to me. Buffalo breath is a terrible thing!

Most of the time, I take off my shoes, so I like to be sure that my socks are pretty fresh. Besides, it's much more comfortable, and better for you, if you remove your shoes. Light slip-on shoes are nice. If you're flying at night and you don't want to disturb the people around you, you might want to bring a portable reading light. (Now our carry-on bag is getting pretty large!)

There's nothing wrong with bringing along a snack. Most of the time they *are* still serving some kind of beverage. Do you want something to read? You might want to bring along whatever you want to read.

Class of Flight

Most of us don't give too much consideration for any class other than economy anymore. The prices for business or first class are out of sight. Nonetheless, sometimes we might have extra money or a special physical need. That would cause us to think about the differences in the seats within economy class among the different airlines. If you go to the SeatGuru site that I've listed below in the tips, you'll find that there are links to information about the seats of virtually every aircraft. The links are on the left side of the page; below is a sample of the first three planes they compare, and they do the same for virtually all the airlines. You also can learn a litte bit about the other amenities in the seating area.

Kind of information available about airline seating

Airline	Aircraft Type	Seat Pitch	Seat Width	Video Type	Laptop Power	Power Type
Air Canada	Airbus A319	31-32"	17"	Overhead TV	Some Seats	AC Power
Same	Airbus A320	Same	Same	Personal TV	Same	Same
Same	Airbus A321	32"	Same	Overhead TV	Same	Same

Arrival

At one point or another, hordes of services and service people are available. I'd say one of the big differences between U.S. airports and foreign airports is first impressions: what you first see and feel when you arrive at a port.

Believe it or not, in the United States, when one arrives even at some of the crazier, larger airports, the arrival is a relatively calm experience. That's also true in certain foreign airports, but what I found for the most part is that there is a kind of busy-ness, and that is characterized by the hordes of individuals working as service personnel, who are looking to help you with your baggage or escort you to land transportation.

While I find the security at foreign airports to be quite good, it may be that because they've been operating at a higher security level than the United States, for many years more, what seems to be a rather casual and easy attitude toward these workers can sometimes be surprising.

It seems like the security people know these boys and young men, so when they intrude across security lines, the security officers often pay little attention. Don't let that throw you too much. I don't think we Americans fully appreciate the tremendous economic impact that tourism has on some of the poorer countries. The local people seem to understand that, and it feels like everyone is aware of and supports individuals who are attempting to make their living from the tourist trade. When you arrive at some of the airports, not only will people want to hustle your bags, but you're also going to see sidewalk sales of all kinds.

The arrival areas of airports are quite passenger friendly, so if you're headed for a hotel or looking for a taxi or limo, there are plenty of signs that will take you to an English-speaking clerk. That person can and will answer any questions a new arrival may have. I frequently find myself going to one of those clerks even if I am not going to use their particular service. They are friendly, not dismissive, and quite happy to help.

Baggage Claim: How to Do It

Obviously, claiming your bags comes before going through customs. All signs lead to the baggage area. Most airports are relatively modern, and they use baggage carousels. The carousels will usually have overhead signs with flight numbers. In international airports, one feature that's a bit different is that they have baggage carts available for arriving passengers (sometimes free, and sometimes for a small fee). The carts are very close to the carousels. Most of the time, I don't have enough luggage to justify a cart; however, because I prefer to travel with others, we will usually collect a cart, grab our bags, and head for customs.

Customs and Immigration

Mostly you can follow the flow of traffic. I find that most customs stations in foreign countries focus their attention on inspecting the luggage of their own citizens rather than that of foreigners. I've never inquired, nor have I made a particular study, but that's the way it seems.

Nine out of ten times, I have never opened a bag. On one occasion I arrived in a Latin American country, and part of the reason I was there was to participate in hosting a major conference. The company with which I was working had prepared a number of personalized pens and conference accessories, which I was transporting. One of the customs officers opened one of those boxes, put on a feigned (though on the surface, genuine) scowl, and in his best demanding voice asked what I was doing with all of that material. I told him, but he seemed unsatisfied. But he was fully satisfied when I gave him samples of each of the items. Somewhat as portrayed in the movies, those customs agents have the power simply to seize anything of yours they like. *They don't choose to … except rarely.* Tourism is so important to those countries that an "incident," were it to become worthy of a newspaper article, could cost them millions of dollars … and they know it.

I think probably the big tip that I can give regarding immigration is this: wait until you're called forward. The process is actually pretty smooth, and virtually all immigration counters have modern computers, and they enter your information quickly, usually with a scanner. They sometimes look at you, and you're on your way.

I'd say that as a general rule, neither customs nor immigration are places to ask questions. They really do just want to move the stream of people along.

Tips

See Resource Pages, page 169 as well as page 110 & 113 for seating diagrams and plane seat configurations.

Chapter 9
Now We're There

(Isn't this what this book is about?)

Attitude/Behavior

Yes, it's back to attitude. Check in with yourself; are you coming into this new land as an eager, joyful guest ... or as an arrogant, expectant customer? I think we're talking here about the difference between entering with a childlike attitude as compared to a childish attitude. So deplane, take your time getting off, walk slowly. Take several deep breaths, get your luggage, get through customs and immigration, and eagerly anticipate next!

Getting to the Hotel

Do you already have transportation arranged for your immediate lodging destination? If you do, that's good. Maybe you're one of those folks who's looking for someone holding a sign that says MR. SMITH, and you can feel important for a moment.

If you haven't made previous arrangements, you should be sure to check with one of the airport folks or at curbside to see if there is a limo from your hotel that you can take for free. Most of us stay at "known" hotels, and they *frequently* provide limo service. I would say that's true far more often than is the case in the United States.

That said, if time and my wallet permit, I really enjoy taking a cab. Ninety percent of cab drivers are very engaging. They are ready and willing to give you a cook's tour en route to your destination. I have never had a cabbie try to take me a long way or by anything but a direct route to my destination. I have had occasion to ask a cabbie to drive me along some side streets or, at my direction, to take me to one place or another en route, and that has always proven to be quite delightful.

One time, in Buenos Aires, our driver took us right through a political demonstration as it was occurring. It was my first real exposure to Latin American demonstrations, and I quickly learned that they are loud and boisterous; according to our standards, they would be close to riotous.

On one occasion, in Guatemala City, the driver explained the history of that capital city, spoke about the mountains in the area, and gave us information about the several major roads that lead to the old capital city and to nearby volcano resort areas, and he recommended a few interesting restaurants. That kind of information made us more interesting guests when we finally met our hosts an hour or two later. It allowed us to ask some intelligent questions about the area and let them know that we were interested.

I can't say too often how important it is to convey interest to your hosts, business associates, or friends in a foreign locale.

Whether it's business or pleasure, it has never failed to cause meetings to be more intimate and productive in a variety of ways.

At some point, you are undoubtedly going to notice a much larger presence of armed military or police. Most countries have an abundance of this, unlike us. You can even get the feeling that the country is under occupation of some kind. Depending on the country, they may have a very different use of the military and of police departments.

It is often the case that the military will perform many of the duties that our police departments perform, thereby explaining some of the greater presence of uniforms. They are also much less "politically correct" when it comes to the display of long arms (shoulder weapons) or smaller automatic weapons. Once you get used to seeing them, you'll find that they're not overbearing or aggressive, but it is something to get used to. Also, it's not terribly rare to see roadblocks and auto inspections.

On the other hand, at nighttime there is far less presence of what we would call police or police patrol. There is much less casual appearance of the police or military at night, and when you do see them, they are often on a mission of some kind. Most countries do not have police cruisers.

Right at the beginning of your trip, perhaps when you first come to your place of lodging, you can establish a few key addresses as "anchor" addresses. Write them down on pieces of paper or cardboard stock, and then make sure that all members of the party have a copy. Phone numbers would be a good addition.

Let's get back to communication. You may not feel it is worthwhile to make a one-time international cell phone purchase as I mentioned above, if you're not going to be away long enough or if you don't travel more than every few years. I would then seriously consider renting a local cell phone. You can usually get one for someplace in the area of $50 for ten days or two weeks, and they usually function very adequately. You will need only one if you're traveling at all times in a single group. If you're going to be traveling in more than one group, it's a great investment for one member of each group to have one. There's nothing more frustrating or scarier than having two groups become separated, confused, or even lost. I've already mentioned several plans for such an event, but I find the cell phone to be the most satisfying. (See Resources pages for country codes, beginning page 159)

It may seem surprising to you that I would suggest that you probably *never* want to drive in most other countries (which is the conservative advice). And you know what? Another thing I found to be a *wonderful* and fairly inexpensive luxury is arranging for a car and a driver ... as in chauffeur! I've been on business trips where it was entirely justified to have a car and driver for the entire day. When there are two, three, or four of you traveling, it doesn't take long for two or three taxi rides to add up to what it would cost you for a driver and a car for the day. In addition, you don't need to have the car and driver for the entire day. They will usually work for a minimum of two or three hours. What does that cost? You can often get a car and a driver for $10 to $12 an hour.

I still remember the name of a driver we used frequently in Buenos Aires: Jorge; and in Paraguay, it was Chi-Chi. Both of them were fine family men whom we got to know and who were invaluable assets, taking us places and explaining things. If you're on vacation rather than conducting business, once again, think about your activities and add up the various tours that you may be taking and at least inquire about the possibility of having a car and a driver. In comparing the cost, I think you might be surprised.

This next subject is a little sensitive, but I'll broach it anyway. It is the subject of the way we walk and look, especially on the street. This is a sensitive subject for several reasons. First, most of us don't want someone or something else dictating *anything* we say or do. Second, it's *very* difficult to change the way we walk or carry ourselves. Third, and I think more importantly, I only want you to briefly consider the possibility of ever being accosted while on the street, as it happens so infrequently. I don't want that consideration to cause worry or fretting. It's a rare thing.

That said, there is wisdom to be exercised—not fear disguised as wisdom, but useful, practical application of knowledge. For instance, why do I want to know what strong-arm robbers say about how they choose victims? That sounds like a strange question, doesn't it? But the answer to that is at the heart of wisdom. People who accost others—whether it is for picking your pocket, stealing your purse, more serious forms of robbery, rape, or even to engage you in a con game—those people size up their victims in an observable and predictable way. We know that because of multiple interviews and studies of imprisoned, convicted accosters.

How to Comport Yourself

Don't worry; in this section, what I want to do is to encourage you to simply be natural ... to be you. It isn't a secret that Americans do less international travel than do the people of many other countries. As we discussed previously, probably the biggest reason is that we are a little isolated, most of that being due to the size of our huge nation. Those who live close to the borders will travel, probably regularly, to either Canada or Mexico. But Europeans have one up on us, don't they?

Think of this: the area of the United States is 3,787,425 square miles, while that of Europe is 3,800,000 square miles.

The entire country of Spain is 194,885 square miles; compare that with California at 163,707 square miles. Italy is 116,324 square miles. France is 211,208 square miles. Texas is 268,601 square miles. What's my point? Is it "Ha ha, look how big the United States is"?

No.

Europeans can—and do—travel by automobile, bicycle, moped, bus, and train from one country to the next with ease and regularity. The European attitude about vacations is that, generally speaking, they plan to travel when they "go on holiday." Much of the time they travel internationally. That's one of the reasons that they speak multiple languages. We shouldn't feel *too* badly because we're so tied to our language. Other countries and other languages are much closer in Europe.

Again, my point is that many other people are more at ease with international traveling than are Americans. Don't let the fact that you may be in a country where you don't understand the language be a daunting and spoiling issue. While I am going to continue to encourage you to learn at least a few words of the local language—we really *can* learn some phrases—still, English is pretty universally spoken and understood. What we want to do with that is not to *demand* or presume on the grace and education of the people who have taken the time to learn our language (that's ugly American stuff), but rather to return the grace, and—with humility—speak relatively slowly, enunciate, and try to avoid idioms and colloquialisms.

Like what? I don't want to make you too paranoid, but think of what someone who doesn't speak English must think when he hears us say that something is "cool," "slick," or "neat." Today, even those words are becoming part of the English-as-a-second-language speaker's vocabulary, but I think you get my point.

I have traveled many times with a good man who, although he's been traveling to Latin America for more than ten years, still speaks almost no Spanish or Portuguese. He maintains several offices in Latin America. Yes, when I travel with him, I sometimes translate for him. Yes, he has even hired translators when he couldn't find someone as fluent as he wanted when he was meeting with different people. However, for the most part, he fends for himself.

Let me share an exciting story about this friend. About ten years ago, he was traveling to Latin America on an exploratory trip for a major American corporation. They were losing business because of sales of counterfeit products. As I've mentioned, much of the counterfeiting of products takes place in China, is exported to Latin America, sometimes remanufactured, sometimes simply labeled and packaged, and then distributed to Latin American consumers and sometimes sent to United States for our consumption.

My friend was on an airplane to Chile. He met an American expatriate who lived most of the time in Chile and owned a business there. The two men began to talk on that long flight. My friend explained a little of what he was doing, and his traveling companion said that because of the business he was in, he was acquainted with some Chilean customs officials who he thought could help my friend.

My friend landed in Santiago, and based on the information he learned on the flight, he traveled to Iquique, located in a rather remote part of Chile, in the far north—considered something of a no man's land—some eight hundred miles north of Santiago. There he contacted some Chilean customs officials, and in a very short time—within several days—ended up seizing the largest seizure of counterfeit product in that corporation's history. Again, my friend speaks no Spanish. I have the photos that document the destruction and burning of those illicit goods.

My friend not only has the nerve to do that (not all of us do), but also he's very comfortable and natural in just about any social environment. It doesn't matter if no one speaks English! He doesn't mind asking right off, "Do you speak English?" Virtually everyone speaks more English than he speaks Spanish, so he's also not shy to point and gesture, and he doesn't get frustrated. Still and all, he makes almost *no* effort to speak their language. He's a rare commodity, because I haven't seen anyone in those foreign countries get offended that he doesn't even try. He seems to be able to project friendliness and a kind of grace that is sensed by people, and on the very rare occasion when he *does* butcher the language in an infrequent effort to speak it, he laughs (not a nervous laughter, but a genuine laughter of good humor), and they laugh along with him, redoubling their own efforts to understand.

I have to admit *my own* frustration when he's asking me to translate for him (a frustration I must admit that the native speakers don't share), because invariably he'll speak with so many colloquialisms that frequently I have to remind him to either rephrase his words or be satisfied with my interpreting the colloquialisms for him. For example, if we've conducted a raid and seized counterfeit products, and we're confronting the individuals in control of those products, we may encounter hostility or resistance, right? In the face of that, my friend might find it necessary to get direct. So what's the easy way to translate, "Tell those pencil-necked turkeys that …" ? Not the easiest thing to translate and either not lose the meaning, or not escalate the situation more than is useful.

What's my point? So much of the success of our travel is based on attitude, and the way we comport and conduct ourselves. You don't have to be as aggressive as the illustration I've given you, but I think you can learn from that example.

What to Wear, and What Not to Wear

This isn't about being appropriately dressed for the weather as much as it is a discussion about how customs of a country will influence the clothing that you choose and pack.

Ladies, the deal is that most cultures are a great deal more modest than we are; blondes still *do* attract a lot of attention; taller women cause heads to turn; virtually everything we see to the contrary are pictures and images that are thrown at us by the advertisers in the different countries who are hoping to appeal to the styles, fashions, and lusts of American travelers.

Sure, we will see small (or no) bathing suits on certain Brazilian and French beaches and a few other places, but unless you're going to go to those particular beaches for that kind of vacation, it is quite different when you start walking around the tourist shopping areas. And please understand that I know about the Caribbean/sunny resort/beach holidays, and those can certainly be fun. I'm talking here about the great majority of *other* places that we will probably be frequenting, such as metropolitan shopping areas, museums, or just walking on the street or in a country village.

If you're going to be spending a part of your travel time in the sunny, bathing-suit environs, take along other clothing that is modest and not so revealing. While their dress habits may be more modest, most Western males are not so modest about their glances, comments, hoots, whistles, pinches, and grabs—except for most Americans (unless you're passing by a construction worksite in Brooklyn). What I'm saying is, our dress and demeanor can—no, *will*—invite attention. Some of it you may not enjoy. Husbands and male friends, kindly and gently encourage your ladies in this area. It may save *you* some discomfort as well!

Where to Go and When

I'm not going to talk here about what tourist attraction to see or not to see. Let's talk for a minute about common sense when it comes to making decisions about where to go in a particular area, or where not to go. When we go to these foreign nations, we may want to make purchases that represent local industry, interests, and values. Let's face it, there *are* some great deals to be had, and you can bring some nice things home *without* taking undue advantage of local labor.

Many times, the best deals are had buying directly from the laborers themselves. Sometimes those laborers are working in the streets, and sometimes those people in the streets who seem to be making their products are really just shills. The desk clerk at your hotel or someone like that can guide you into making that decision. I wouldn't always rely on a taxi driver; as you might suspect, they will have their own deals with some of the vendors and will try to steer you toward them. *That isn't always bad.* We once bought some beautiful rugs in Morocco, being fully aware that our tour guide had steered us deep into Tangiers and that he was participating in business with the shop. But it's good to know that kind of information up front.

On a more practical note, frequently you can be taken to the manufacturer's place of business (sometimes their home); just know that just as frequently it is going to be a poorer area of town. Be wise in selecting when you go, with whom, and how much money you take.

What's Wise, and What Isn't?

Well, this is probably another very controversial section. What we're talking about is what is wise to do (travel or not, go here or go there, eat this or eat that), and that can be such a subjective decision. Many or most advisory bulletins, letters, or websites are fed and prepared by local news reports or by talking with the press in the United States. The information fed into those sources is *not* typically coming from people who are trained observers with the skills and experience to translate that information into relatively valid, at least semi-objective, common-sense observations.

Simply put, most information going into the "advisory" sites is coming from reporters, who may tend to report information with a goal toward selling news. I know it may shock some of you to hear that reporters (and the vehicles through which they report) are all about selling their product. Truth, objectivity, and common sense may not be at the forefront of their reports.

It's one thing to report a tornado or earthquake or tidal wave, along with photographs, and attempt to give the factual information about damage and loss. In those situations, there is a substantial body of confirmable information that will be scrutinized by a variety of different reporters, which will tend to make the reporting of that information pretty objective.

On the other hand, the reporting of crime or economics, for instance, can be presented in a variety of ways so as to influence the reader or listener or viewer to view a whole area, nation, or continent a certain way. Let me cite an example right here in the United States. Let's take two cities in New York: Rochester and New York City. Where's the highest murder rate? New York City, right? (This is a trick question, and you're probably trying to guess the answer!) Yes, the murder rate in Rochester is four times higher than that of New York City. New York City had 539 homicides in 2005; Rochester had fifty-three in 2005. New York City has a population of 8,116,000, which means a homicide rate of one for every 15,057 people; Rochester has a population of 212,000, which results in a ratio of one homicide for every four thousand people.

Depending on where you live, the politics (governmental and newspaper), and the individual reporter, the way that information is broadcast can have a significant impact on tourism and budgets. Think of how the headlines could read in New York City, with about one and a half murders per day occurring.

So when we're traveling internationally, what will we be warned about? We will be warned about terrorism, kidnappings, maybe purse snatchings, carjackings, and sometimes pickpocketing and hotel burglaries. Secondary kinds of reporting will include riots or demonstrations, particularly those being held about or against the United States.

I'm going to go out on a limb here and suggest that most of the riots and demonstrations are going to be conducted against our *government* and not against us as individuals. They very, very rarely consist of angry crowds carrying sticks and looking for Americans to beat. As I've mentioned, I've never altered my travel plans based on anti-American sentiments.

Here's *my* warning. Please don't check your brain at the door. Right now, for example, the United States is at war in Iraq and certain other places in the Middle East and Far East. As of July 2009 for instance, don't go to Afghanistan as a tourist! Don't go to those several African nations where there is open civil war and bloodshed in the streets! Don't go to a country that has suffered from a tsunami within the last several weeks! Is that hard to figure out? Virtually every other place you can decide about on an individual basis by going to a variety of websites, as an example, and by getting your news from a broad range of sources. In Chapter 4, I've provided some newspaper sources. Remember, they're selling newspapers. Most have English editions. I kind of like listening to the BBC (the British Broadcasting Company). While they are our friends, they often provide a slightly different perspective on the news.

Go to some of the tourism websites, and write them questions about the area. Sure, they're going to give you glowing reports, but it won't take much to read between the lines. Contact a couple of local hotels; send them email asking them about local conditions. Ask them, for example, if you can take nighttime strolls around their area or downtown. They are usually pretty straightforward in responding to those kinds of questions. They don't want to hurt their own businesses. Now, I would also say that people in a number of the areas to which we will travel are going to suggest that we don't take unaccompanied nighttime strolls in certain areas. Because I've learned that these different sources are pretty straightforward, I tend to give their advice a lot of credit, mixed with other information I've gathered; and I've found it to be true, but as I've mentioned too many times already, I've not had to cancel or even alter plans very much.

Maps: Know Your Route, Whether Walking or Riding

We've kind of covered this topic, haven't we? It's very, very easy to get relatively decent maps for free online. Unless you have a personal interest in knowing detailed information about the area—for instance, if you are taking a multi-country tour, and you like being able to follow your progress—then you're going to be able to find local maps, which you can easily print, that will do you quite well.

I have a couple of large atlases sitting on my shelf, and I use them to remind myself about the overall perspective of an area. I also have a shelf of fairly expensive maps of countries and continents, almost none of which I've used, because I have those smaller, quite adequate maps (and they're sometimes more up to date). But at the time of my travel, I wanted to have that $10 foldout map, and to be quite honest, I probably wouldn't have been dissuaded from buying it. Once again, I'm just telling you what my experience has been. I hope it's obvious that if you are driving someplace, then you'd want a nice, complete map.

During Your Travels, Who Will Help You Most, and Quickest?

First, let me say that I have suggested that you have certain contact information in your possession when you travel. Please have that with you. It may be good to have the address and phone number of the American embassy; it *will* be good to have the address and phone number of your hotel, and of any businesses or friends with whom you'll be visiting.

Now, should you need help relatively quickly, to whom should you turn? If someone is bleeding, the answer is going to be obvious, I hope. But if you're looking for directions, or are lost, or are confused, or maybe just want some general information, I'd really suggest looking for a friendly merchant. Walking off the street into a small shop or department store can really result in a very happy exchange of information. I am not recommending against contacting a policeman or other public servant; sometimes they too can be very helpful. But overall, I find merchants and businesspeople to be the most available, the most ready, and the most willing. You can even pop into a hotel in which you are *not* lodging and ask questions.

Another good source—one frequently overlooked—is phone books. You can look in phone books that you can't read because of the language barrier, and invariably you'll be able to spot some English-named corporation listed. Large corporations like that always have English speakers on their staffs. Don't feel like you can't call them, especially if you're feeling urgent about something.

Eating and Drinking

Eating preferences aside, frequently you are going to wonder where it is safe to eat, as far as hygiene is concerned. One issue of concern is what the local custom or habit of the country may be. If you're going to a country where you know that eating cats is a delicacy, that's going to be one factor in your decision-making process, isn't it?

But most of us don't go to those places, so we can drill down a little bit about how to make those choices. You *do* have to use some common sense. Yes, there are some areas where you don't want to drink the water. You'll be able to find out that kind of information before you go, and you'll be able to take precautions appropriately. For the most part, you're going to use the same criteria for selecting a foreign eating place as you would here in the United States. You're going to have to make mental adjustments for what may be less availability of modern equipment, or less emphasis upon up-to-date restaurant furnishings. In foreign countries, I find a greater use of linens in restaurants than here in the United States.

Tips

For radio sites and information sources, see the Bonus Material (see back cover for instructions on how to obtain your Bonus Materials).

Chapter 10
What If? (Things Do Happen)

We don't want to dwell more than, say, half an hour on the subject, but we'll talk about it anyway. Let's consider what some of the options are, if everything turns upside down.

First, the U.S. embassy is a very useful resource. I have found—for the most part—that they are willing to help. They frequently have hired locals to help staff the embassy, and these individuals can assist with not only emergency questions but also practical help. *Be equipped with the address and phone number of the embassy.* It is *very* useful to know.

Again, in the instance of literally being somewhere on the street and getting lost or separated, you will find much help in the local citizenry. Store owners are usually stable, good citizens. Most government officials are the same. Make contact with someone you deem to be a stable person, and then worry about whether they speak English or not. Most shop owners, especially in tourist areas, speak some English. They often have children of their own, in their shops, who may speak fluent English. Virtually all travel organizations, including taxi services, airlines, trains, buses, tour guides, and boats, either have English speakers or all employees speak some English. Financial institutions have English speakers. School teachers and health-care providers often speak English. What if you find no English speakers at all? Rudimentary hand signing will do the trick.

Next, there are emergency plans…simple, easily filled out.

Emergency Family Plan

Make sure your family has a plan in case of an emergency. Before an emergency happens, sit down together and decide how you will get in contact with each other, where you will go, and what you will do in an emergency. Keep a copy of this plan in your emergency supply kit or another safe place where you can access it in the event of an emergency.

Out of town contact name:

Telephone number:

E-mail:

Neighborhood Meeting Place:

Telephone number:

Regional Meeting Place:

Telephone number:

Evacuation Location:

Telephone number:

Fill out the following information for each family member and keep it up to date. *Make a copy of each person's passport so as to have a photo on hand.*

Name:

Social Security Number:

Date of Birth:

Important Medical Info:

There are also a variety of other publications that are at least worth reading. Among them are the following:

1) The Family Emergency Plan (see above; offered as a PDF file online)
2) Passport Security (a discussion about protecting and safeguarding the passport)
3) Personal Security at Home (also a PDF)
4) Security Business Travelers
5) Security of American Families Abroad
6) Security Guideline for Children Abroad

All of these are U.S. State Department publications available for free. (See the Bonus Material offered on the website, www.secretsfortravelsurvival.com)

Chapter 11
A Walk Through from
Two Recent Trips: England and Italy

What I Learned

Okay, so the timing of this trip was something of a bonus for me! This was a family trip that had been planned for some months. The circumstances surrounding it bear telling because they directly influenced—perhaps more than usual—the planning and the results.

Our second daughter is now twenty-three years old, and we're grateful that she is still at home. Our second son is now almost nineteen years old, and we talked for some time about taking a trip with all the family together, before the remaining two move out and begin to pursue life away from home. As homeschoolers, we spent a considerable amount of time over the years on ancient classic literature, history, and culture.

We decided that what we wanted to do was to travel to England to see our older daughter and family, who are currently living in Bristol. From there, we thought that taking a trip to Greece would be wonderful because of the study and pleasure taken in that country. My wife, Maryann, began several months in advance of our departure (early April 2007) searching for flights that would take us where and when we wanted at the best rates. We planned to spend a week and a half in England and about a week and a half in Greece. The plans were set; flights were reserved and paid for, and hotels were reserved and paid for.

Just a couple of months before our departure, Maryann was contacted by a man in Italy who said he was a relative on her father's side. He had spent years on the family genealogy, and his search had taken him to the United States, where several of his uncles and aunts had emigrated, starting in the early 1900s. He had sent letters and several hundred email messages to other relatives, with virtually no response. And to add lemon juice to the paper cut, there was both intrigue and mystery surrounding the story, and—as we later found out—even a murder!

Pasquale learned that we were coming to Europe, heard that our trip included Greece, and he passionately rose up and semi-lightheartedly protested vigorously, saying that it would be crazy to go to Greece when we could go to Italy, meet them, stay with them, and let him drive us around. With such an impassioned presentation, how could we not?

Because the flights and hotels had already been reserved and paid for, Maryann set out to see what she could do and whether it would even be possible. Normally we would make these sorts of changes online, but Maryann found out that, as is so often the case, speaking directly with the airlines and hotels was the only way to go. She pled our case, telling them exactly what had happened. Because we generally expect to operate within the favor of God and man, the results were exciting and even surprising. We were able to change everything, obtain reasonable flights to Rome, and change hotel accommodations, and the total changes at this relatively last-minute time only cost us an additional $200. (In fact, we probably ended up saving, because of the time that we spent with our newfound relatives.)

So yes, we did our own checking and confirmed that Pasquale was a part of a branch of the family tree that most here in the United States had barely even considered. It was sad, in a way. Off we went, traveling through Philadelphia to Gatwick Airport in London, where we rented a car and I drove on the wrong side of the road to Bristol and thence to Devon, where we rented a country cottage near the ocean. It was an outstanding time!

Here are a couple of observations for this leg of the trip. First off, security exiting the United States was smooth. What I realized again is that while most carriers are using similar or the same aircraft, with predictable under-the-seat and overhead space, the fee policies of the different airlines do very somewhat, especially in foreign countries.

Following most of my own advice helped us to be relatively well prepared. As far as **packing** was concerned, each of the four of us took a relatively large check-on suitcase, and each of us planned to take one carry-on as well. One carry-on seemed to be the most conservative standard of each of the airlines with which we checked. In other words, some airlines would allow more than one carry-on, but we had to remember that we would have to travel in accordance with what the most conservative carrier would allow. (Or we would have to be willing to stuff an extra bag in the check-on luggage.)

I continue to recommend wheels for virtually every **bag** that you carry, perhaps with the exception of the ladies' purses. I was pleased with a carry-on bag (such as a computer bag with extra space), and I will recommend that it be as close to nine inches deep as is possible. Yes, you can exceed that somewhat, depending on the aircraft, but I found that nine inches would make it overhead or under the seat in every instance. I wore my camera bag on my belt, and I attached that to my carry-on bag while going through security. I identified one pocket in my carry-on bag where I would put everything I could possibly put that was in my pockets or on my wrist, so as to make going through as easy as possible. Again, that proved to be a very effective method. The policy for removing belts and/or shoes through security varied and was extremely inconsistent. I also continue to recommend slip-on shoes and an easily removed belt.

I used the closable plastic bag method for packing my check-on luggage. As silly a detail as it may seem, I can't overemphasize what a good method this is. I use the commercially produced resealable plastic bags. You can roll your clothes or fold them, and you can place them inside the bag, and it flattens to the maximum and maintains a darned good press on the clothes. Is there a drawback? A slight one, yes: packing that way makes your clothing so compact that because you get far more in your suitcase, it becomes a little heavier. That's the worst part of it.

Let's talk for a minute about **modes of travel.** Mostly, we're going to be traveling by air, right? This reminder is as applicable here in the United States as it is overseas, but it bears brief discussion. In your search for tickets, be aware that there are many local airlines, many of which are unadvertised, so we want to search carefully. When we were in London and in Rome, we noticed eight or ten local airlines that we could use, and they were all what you would call "economy mode" airlines. But they also mostly used new aircraft, and they were very competitive pricewise. Probably because of the marketing strategies of the Internet, they're not as easy to find; however, we found many of them advertising with the country or city chambers of commerce.

Here is a list from LowCostAirlinesEurope.org:
(Remember: this list is in constant flux!)

1. <u>Aegean Airlines</u> – Flights within Greece (home base) and Greece to Western Europe
2. <u>Aer Arann</u> – Flights within Ireland and from Ireland to England, Scotland
3. <u>Air 2000</u> – Flights between England (home base Manchester) and Portugal, Spain
4. <u>Air Baltic</u> – Flights between home bases Riga (Latvia), Vilnius (Lithuania) and Austria, Belarus, Belgium, Czech Rep., Denmark, Estonia, Finland, Germany, Ireland, Netherlands, Poland, Russia, Sweden, Ukraine
5. <u>Air Berlin</u> – Flights within Germany and from Germany (home base Berlin) to Austria, Cyprus, Egypt, England, Greece, Italy, Morocco, Portugal, Spain, Tunisia, Turkey
6. <u>Air Finland</u> – Flights within Finland (home base Helsinki) and from Finland to France, Italy, Spain
7. <u>Air Scotland</u> – Flights between Scotland (home base) and Spain
8. <u>Air Service Plus</u> – Flights between Italy (home base Pescara) and Brussels, Paris
9. <u>Air Southwest</u> – Flights within England
10. <u>Alpi Eagles</u> – Flights within Italy (home base Venice)
11. <u>Baboo</u> – Flights between Switzerland (home base Geneva) and Czech Rep., France, Italy, Spain
12. <u>BelleAir</u> – Flights from Italy to Albania, Greece, Turkey

13. <u>Blue1</u> – Flights within Finland and from Finland (home base Helsinki) to Belgium, Denmark, Germany, Netherlands, Norway, Sweden

14. <u>Blue Air</u> – Flights between Romania (home base) and France, Germany, Italy, Netherlands, Spain, Turkey

15. <u>Blue-Express</u> – Flights within Italy and Italy (home base Rome) to Austria, France, Germany, Libya

16. <u>BMI Baby</u> – Flights between England (home base) and Czech Rep., France, Germany, Ireland, Italy, Portugal, Spain, Switzerland, Wales

17. <u>British European</u> – Flights between England and Channel Islands, France, Ireland, Isle of Man, Italy, Netherlands, Scotland, Spain, Switzerland, Ulster

18. <u>BudgetAir</u> – Flights between Ireland (home base Dublin) and France, Greece, Portugal, Spain

19. <u>CentralWings</u> – Flights between Poland (home base) and Czech Rep., England, Germany, Italy, Malta, Spain

20. <u>Clickair</u> – Flights between Spain (home base Barcelona) and Czech Rep., France, Germany, Ireland, Italy, Netherlands, Portugal, Switzerland

21. <u>Condor</u> – Flights from Germany to most European countries

22. <u>Corendon</u> – Flights between Netherlands and Turkey

23. <u>Dau Air</u> – Flights between Germany (home base Dortmund) and Poland, Switzerland

24. <u>EasyJet</u> – Flights between England (home base London) and Denmark, France, Greece, Netherlands, Scotland, Spain, Switzerland, Ulster

25. <u>Evolavia</u> – Flights between Italy (home base Ancona) and France, Russia, Spain

26. <u>Excel Airways</u> – Flights from England and Scotland to Egypt, France, Greece, Malta, Portugal, Spain, Turkey

27. <u>Fare4U</u> – Flights between Malta (home base) and London Stansted

28. <u>Fly Dba</u> – Flights within Germany and from Germany to France, Spain
29. <u>Fly Me</u> – Flights within Sweden (home base) and Finland
30. <u>German Wings</u> <u>Fake low-cost by Lufthansa?</u> <u>Read here</u> <u>Latest news about German Wings</u> Flights within Germany and from Germany (home base Cologne) to Austria, Czech Republic, England, France, Hungary, Italy, Portugal, Spain, Switzerland and Turkey
31. <u>Globespan</u> – Flights between Scotland (home base) and France, Italy, Spain
32. <u>Hapag Lloyd Express</u> – Flights within Germany (home base Cologne-Bonn) and from Germany to England, France, Italy, Spain
33. <u>Helvetic Airways</u> – Flights between Switzerland (home base Zurich) and Austria, Belgium, Spain
34. <u>Iceland Express</u> – Flights between Iceland (home base) and Denmark, England
35. <u>InterSky</u> – Flights between Austria (home base Wien) and France, Italy, Switzerland
36. <u>Itali Airlines</u> – Flights within Italy and Italy - Croatia v.v.
37. <u>Jet2</u> – *Warning: Very slow loading home page!* Flights between England (home base Leeds-Bradford) and France, Italy, Netherlands, Spain
38. <u>LTU</u> - Flights from Germany to most European countries
39. <u>Meridiana</u> – Flights within Italy (home base Florence) and from Italy to England, France, Italy, Netherlands, Spain
40. <u>Monarch Airlines</u> – Flights between England (home base London-Luton) and Gibraltar, Portugal, Spain
41. <u>My Travel Lite</u> – Flights between England (home base) and France, Portugal, Spain, Switzerland
42. <u>MyAir - My Way Airlines</u> – Flights within Italy and between Italy (home base) and France, Romania and Spain
43. <u>Nordic Airlink</u> – *Warning: Very slow loading home page!* Flights between Sweden (home base Stockholm) and Norway

44. <u>Norwegian Air Shuttle</u> – Flights within Norway (home base) and from Norway to England, Portugal, Spain
45. <u>Pegasus Airlines</u> – Flights within Turkey and Turkey - Germany v.v.
46. <u>Ryanair</u> – Flights between England (home base London-Stansted) and Austria, Belgium, Denmark, Finland, France, Germany, Ireland, Italy, Netherlands, Norway, Portugal, Scotland, Spain, Sweden
47. <u>Scandjet</u> – Flights between Sweden (home base) and Bosnia, Croatia
48. <u>SkyEurope</u> – *Warning: Very slow loading home page!* Flights between Slovakia (home base Bratislava) and Croatia, Czech Republic, England, France, Italy, Germany, Netherlands, Poland, Spain, Switzerland
49. <u>Smart Wings</u> – Flights between Czech Republic (home base Prague) and Denmark, France, Netherlands, Spain, Switzerland
50. <u>Snalskjutsen</u> – Flights within Sweden (home base) and from Sweden to France, Ireland, Italy, Scotland
51. <u>SnowFlake Airlines</u> – Flights from Denmark (home base Copenhagen) and Sweden (home base Stockholm) to Czech Rep., France, Greece, Hungary, Ireland, Italy, Spain, Turkey
52. <u>Sterling</u> – Flights between Denmark (home base Copenhagen) and France, Greece, Italy, Madeira, Norway, Spain, Sweden
53. <u>Sun Express</u> – Flights between Turkey (home base Antalya) and Austria, Germany, Switzerland
54. <u>ThomsonFly</u> – Flights between England (home base Coventry) and France, Italy, Jersey, Spain
55. <u>Transavia</u> – *Warning: Very slow loading home page!* Flights between Netherlands (home base Amsterdam) and Denmark, England, France, Germany, Ireland, Italy, Norway, Portugal, Spain, Sweden
56. <u>Virgin Express</u> - Flights between Belgium (home base Brussels) and Denmark, England, France, Greece, Italy, Portugal, Spain, Sweden, Switzerland
57. <u>VLM Airlines</u> - Flights between Belgium (home base) and England, Germany, Guernsey, Italy, Jersey, Luxembourg and Netherlands

58. Vueling Airlines - Flights within Spain (home base) and from Spain to Brussels, Paris
59. Windjet Vola - Flights within Italy (home base Sicily)
60. Wizz Air – Flights from Hungary (home base Budapest) and Poland (home base Katowice) to Czech Rep., England, France, Greece, Germany, Italy, Spain and Sweden

We saw many of these. Check them out, though, before booking. These lines are *not* easy to locate, and they are not advertised frequently. How do you check them out?

Several ways. Do an inquiry through the Internet. Remember, the Internet sometimes has truthful information! You can follow the Web search with queries through travel agents or by questioning any friends who have traveled.

What else?

Let's talk some more taxi talk. Increasingly, we found that many of the major airports have fixed rates (maximum ceilings) for some taxis that ferry between the airport and the central part of the particular city. In many cities, you can walk from the airport terminal out to the curb by the taxi stand, and there will be a sign that indicates the maximum permissible fee to be charged by the taxi from the airport to the central portion of the city—for instance, to Rome. Be aware that there are private taxis—taxis that aren't part of the numerous contracted taxi companies for that service—and those cabs aren't constrained by a fixed rate. During our travel, those kinds of taxis identified themselves as such. Another factor to consider is that when there is a fixed rate from the airport to the city, that may also be affected by the size and/or number of pieces of luggage that you have. The four of us had a total of eight pieces of luggage, even though four of them were carry-ons. Because of the smaller size of vehicles in general, and of taxis specifically, there are a number of instances when we literally couldn't fit in one taxicab, so indeed we had to take advantage of those unregulated taxis. They were often larger vehicles or vans. So be aware that this phenomenon occurs, and don't be shy about asking or refusing the service of a taxi that is offered to you … no matter how big the driver's smile.

Look for the M

Let's discuss some logistics once in the city. I realize that I didn't talk much about metropolitan mass or rapid transit. I'd like to correct that now, and I will use as an example our experience in Rome.

We stayed in a hotel that was relatively central to Rome. Quite by chance, the hotel was located not far from the main rapid-transit terminal—in this instance, a subway. On about the third day in Rome, having walked thousands of miles, we began to look at the convenience and pricing of the subway. We were pleasantly surprised! For about four dollars apiece per day, we could travel

Buying Tokens

throughout the subway system as frequently as we wanted.

The map of the Rome subway system, shows a system that services the central part of Rome, mainly. For about $16 per week, one could have that privilege.

Taxis are expensive and gasoline is expensive, and these systems are pretty user-friendly. They mostly have at least dual-language signs, including English. We thoroughly

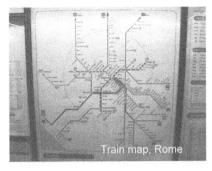
Train map, Rome

enjoyed being able to hop on the subway, travel a mile or two, get off for as long as we wanted to see a site, and then get back on and go to the next. All that said, I would also recommend extensive walking, for that is where you pick up the atmosphere and flavor of the community. This kind of information is almost always available on the Internet, and you should consider finding it in advance of your trip. You can save money and energy.

As for **automobile travel**, as I've mentioned before, for the most part I'd prefer not to rent a vehicle and drive. Mostly, when driving, you miss out on a great deal of the scenery, not to speak of having to concentrate on a different

Turnstile to Rome metro

kind of driving and the local highway designs. Fuel was about eight dollars a gallon in Europe. Happily, distances aren't so far that extensive driving is necessary. When in England, we rented

Inside Italian train

a diesel-powered vehicle, and with it we got about forty-six miles per gallon, even though it was a station wagon. In that instance, it was great to have a vehicle to drive. Once again, if you're going to consider renting a vehicle, do a quick search online. There are many, many companies that rent automobiles, most of which we'd never heard of. We were very pleased with the company we found online.

In Rome, as in many cities, the train terminal is also the subway/metro terminal. We crossed Italy from Rome to Foggia, about a three-and-a-half-hour train ride. The trains were fast, clean, and on time, and it's not a bad way to see the countryside. Most of them offer at least two classes. We chose first class, which was only another $15 per ticket above coach. We found that the main difference was a small amount of legroom (economy legroom was quite adequate) and a little better accommodation for luggage, of which we took advantage.

First and foremost, remember that there is only the very most fundamental, basic similarity in airport security policies and procedures not only internationally, but also within our own country. I almost completely forgot that, having been a little more accustomed to it than the rest of my family. It seemed that exiting our country was less of a problem than returning.

Second but related to the first, don't ever try to make sense of what's going on! There are some basic procedures, which are outlined and discussed especially in Chapters 7 and 8. Pay attention to those suggestions and be prepared—without predicting unusual, senseless, or even foolish happenings in the security world—and things will go swimmingly well.

For example, I think I mentioned that during the last few years, I've taken to wearing a sport jacket, even if with Levis and a T-shirt. It's not only a convenient way to carry your coat and have it come out in relatively good shape, it also seems to lend an air of "class" in the minds of some security personnel, especially during this trip.

For some reason, the "return legs" provided some airport security challenges. We had to fly from Rome to London and then from London to the United States. Coming from the Philadelphia airport back to New York, the line through security was particularly long. When we all arrived at the point where you are directed to a particular lane, the security person looked at me and directed me to a lane that was being used exclusively for a late flight on American Airlines. We were flying USAir. That line moved along quickly, and I ended up making it through security ten to fifteen minutes more quickly than the rest of my family. We figured out that my sport coat made me look like one of the businesspeople that was on that American flight. (It looked like a business group.)

Another interesting thing happened in Rome. Prior to the actual security check, airport security had established a pre-check. The first one was checking to be sure that no one had fluids or nonprescription medications, and they noticed that each of us had not only a carry-on bag but also some other small accessory—in my case, a small video camera in its own case. My wife had a full-size purse. They pulled us both out of line and requested that we put the accessory items in our carry-on bags. When we voiced the mildest question (not complaint), they became agitated and angry.

We complied, however, for both of our carry-on bags expanded considerably beyond the permissible size for a carry-on bag. In fact, at the second checkpoint, there was a metal frame that was intended to be the measuring device for carry-ons, in order to ensure that they did not exceed the maximum size. So we put the items into our carry-on bags, and we made it through the first security checkpoint. And as we were walking to the second one, we removed those accessory bags in order to have our carry-ons comply with the carry-on size. At the second checkpoint, there was no objection to the extra accessory bags. Go figure!

At this point in our traveling lives, we have to make the decision to not view airport security as the enemy. Really, at virtually all stages of our travel en route, we have to plan to keep things as simple as possible. Have your ID and/or your passport quickly available. Have your boarding pass quickly available. **Remember**: while you want to have them quickly available, you don't want them to be accessible to others. Here are some considerations:

- Take one check-on bag and one carry-on. Make the carry-on no thicker than about nine inches. It's best if it can roll on wheels.
- Use some kind of sealable plastic bag to pack your clothes.
- Don't forget at least one voltage/plug accessory
- Take along a nice digital camera with plenty of memory. (It's cheap!)
- Plan for sufficient time between flights, if connecting.
- Carry along any maps, for a big airport and for the major cities.
- I'd use plastic instead of money. There's a good exchange rate. But get maybe $50 of the local currency at the airport, when first arriving. You'll always use it.
- Don't be afraid to ask, or even challenge, regarding prices, whether for taxis or meals. (Oh, on that point, many countries add the gratuity onto the bill and may "forget" to inform you of that. Ask!)

Bogotá, Colombia

This beautiful, romantic, resource-rich country has had its problems over the last several decades, indeed. Be of good cheer! Much has changed in the last several years, and with only the slightest word of caution, I'd say it is one of the best bargains going for the traveler—not simply from an economic standpoint, although it may be slightly lower in cost than traveling in the United States, but rather from the standpoint of accommodations, conveniences, eating, warmth and welcoming of culture and society, things to do, and natural resources. This is a place to consider.

Business took me there for most of two weeks at the end of July and into August 2007. If you have paid even slight attention to the international news over the years, you will have in the back of your mind the news about active drug cartels, smuggling, and civil war; you may have some vague recollection of hearing of a militant group known as FARC, an acronym translated several different ways, but meaning "the Armed Revolutionary Forces of Colombia." You've heard of bombings, kidnappings, even some running gun battles. Go to Colombia? No way!

Before my trip, I sat with a number of executives of the company who had the problem in Bogotá. The meeting opened with someone saying, "I want everyone making this trip armed!" The sentiment to keep everyone safe, accompanied by the thought that Colombia is a dangerous place, was expressed loud and clear. I was to travel to Bogotá and meet an associate, who was coming in from another Latin American country, and with whom I'd be partnering. We had an in-country group of investigators and security personnel with whom we'd worked in the past, and who had proven themselves reliable and efficient.

We arranged for around-the-clock escorts (some armed) for several other consultants who would also be joining us. My partner had done some advance work and had gotten updated on the social, political, and criminal activities and trends, and we determined that we would not need bodyguards, armored cars, or "chase cars" (those escort vehicles that follow behind) for ourselves.

My partner was scheduled to arrive in Bogotá around noon. Arrangements were made for us to stay at a particular hotel, and we arranged to use the conference room of another hotel several blocks away for interviews, just as a safety precaution. My partner arranged for a car and driver from the hotel to meet me at the airport. I was due in around 1:30 PM.

I arrived a bit late. I made it to the luggage area, and for perhaps the first time ever, my luggage didn't arrive. I'd had a connecting flight in New York City, which had been close. (Remember: figure in time for delays between flights, especially international ones. I like a solid hour between arrival time and connection departure, depending on the airport. Perhaps more.) I had needed to hustle a bit to make my connection. Usually, luggage is faster connecting, so I didn't worry when my own connecting time was "close" (is that what running and keeping the passenger door open beyond the usual time is?). So I was surprised about the luggage lag. However, even worse was the fact that the driver from the hotel and my partner were anticipating my arrival on schedule. The plane did arrive on time, but they couldn't see the passengers departing, and they had to wait some distance away from the luggage area. The bottom line was that they weren't sure I'd been on the plane. The airline personnel were very cooperative. But after an hour and a half, I still had no luggage. It might be in on a late evening flight, they said, and told me to call.

Another first for me was that this time, I had decided to put some of my equipment in the checked baggage. I usually don't, in the event that luggage might be lost, stolen, or misplaced. This time I checked some important but not mission-critical equipment.

Happily, the driver and my partner had waited. (Let's call my partner "S." This person has traveled and worked around the world, still does the same, and needs not to be compromised!) We drove to our hotel and settled in. Does this look like your typical hotel?

There are many such smaller "boutique" hotels in Bogotá, and the design comes from the many years of instability due to the high-crime profile of the city. Look at the exterior. It looks more like an office building. The carport allows one car at a time; it has a

Secure hotel, Bogotá

U-shaped drive and a locked front door with security in the form of doormen. It has maybe twenty-five rooms. It was very nice accommodation, with wireless Internet access and a fine breakfast included.

We walked out the door and went to our left, and two blocks down was a lovely square, around which were dozens of wonder-

Outdoor café, Bogotá

ful open-air patio cafes. A short taxi ride away, in the old town area near the old opera house, you can still see vestiges of yesteryear, when street violence was quite frequent. But look closely at the faces of these soldier-policemen: they are smiling and are thought of much as we think of our patrol officers standing on the corners in, say, New York City.

Street patrol, Bogotá, Colombia

Happily, "S" knew the way around Bogotá and had many contacts and friends. The benefit for me was that I had the experience of a well-seasoned person with whom to work and travel, who knew where to go in one of the largest, most busy cities in the world. "S" knows the various districts of Bogotá and knew of local shopping and eating spots. I don't think I could have traveled and worked better than I did. "S" and I worked sixteen to eighteen hours a day. We interviewed dozens of people, meeting with government officials and high-society and lower society people. We eventually found several individuals who worked with the target of our investigation. With their help, we developed a list of approximately a dozen violations committed by this individual. "S" helped orchestrate a successful investigation, the details of which would make a great movie! All the elements were there: corruption, betrayal, theft, sex, and intrigue, and the subject confessed!

Through it all, this beautiful city, once at the top of most lists of "most dangerous cities in the world," treated us well. Remember, we weren't traveling as VIPs when we were out and about in the city. Yes, when important individuals were brought in for the culmination of the investigation, we provided security escorts ... for them. But all the rest of the time, we were as any other tourists. I just had the good fortune to be with an experienced and wise companion who made all the difference in our trip, in all ways! *I can be that person for you.*

So ... what have I learned? What can I pass on to you? The trip to Bogotá reinforced the value in doing some reasonable research in advance of the trip. I spent a few hours online; I made a few phone calls. Yes, I may have easily accessed people and sources, but even through them I only confirmed information that was publicly and readily available. You can do that too.

Please consider the following:

- If you need or desire to travel somewhere but hear it's not a good place to go, for whatever reason, don't ignore the warnings; check it all out. I've provided ample information for you to do that.

- Plan ahead. Research. Pack well. Consider what you really will use.

- Be wise about what you do and where you go. But again, once there, ask a couple of different people about the place you're thinking of going. Your tour guide is someone to whom to listen. Or ask the desk clerk at an established hotel, or call the local American embassy. They will be conservative in their advice, but they may actually provide useful information. Think about it: a taxi driver, or someone who could benefit from referring you to a business—or even set you up for a crime—isn't the person to ask.

- Think about what you are wearing. This can go for both genders. Without being negative, we Americans can be pretty thoughtless when it comes to dress. Never intending to offend, we might dress for comfort or for "splash," not realizing that we could be violating local custom ... or in rare cases, local law.

- Stretch a bit. Consider eating some exotic local food … upon good advice, of course. Buy a local piece of art, a bauble, or some clothing "When in Rome, do as the Romans do." Good sense applies!
- Print some of the tips, charts, or forms that have been made available.
- Attitude makes all the difference in the world.

Late Update

The latest innovation by the Transportation Security Administration is the introduction of three different passenger lanes for passing through the security process. One lane is for expert and experienced travelers; one lane is for families; the third lane is for "casual" travelers. It is still too early to determine if this is going to smooth the process. At this point, there is no real guide as to what each lane really means. The family lane is kind of self explanatory, but what's the difference between the expert and casual traveler? I like the idea, though, that TSA is attempting to be innovative.

In addition, many airports are now providing a free parking zone…sometimes near, sometimes not so near the airport… called "Cell Phone Parking" or similar name. This is meant to be a convenience for individuals who are picking up or dropping off passengers. In the event a flight is delayed, greeters and meters can wait in the "Cell Phone" lot until contacted by their passenger, then they can pull up to curbside and retrieve passengers and luggage.

It seems those "puff" machines used to detect explosives may be less popular. If you have a choice, don't go through them. It's usually voluntary, but often slows the process way down

Resource Pages

Following are resources you can easily copy and print for taking along

ALL LINKS TO INTERNET SOURCES

Chapter 2

General/global information

1) http://t21.ca/ an overall "global" and heavily Africa view.
2) http://www.eurodad.org/default.aspx European economics
   also: http://www.worldbank.org/
   http://www.un.org/aroundworld/map/ (UN organizations)
3) The U.S. Department of State, especially
   a. http://www.ds-osac.org/
   b. http://travel.state.gov
4) http://www.un.org/english/ United Nations
5) http://www.who.int/en/ World Health Organization
6) http://www.infoplease.com/countries.html Countries of the
   world --- more up to date on current events than #7
7) https://www.cia.gov/cia/publications/factbook/index.html
   This CIA source is not bad
8) (http://www.flyingtigersvideo.com/
9) http://www.bbc.co.uk/aste

Chapter 4

News and information

http://library.uncg.edu/news/
http://www.onlinenewspapers.com/
http://en.wikipedia.org/wiki/Country
http://www.theworldisnotflat.com/tags/customs
http://www.subscription-offers.com/magazines/arthur-frommers-
   budget/
http://www.frommers.com/
http://world.altavista.com/

Chapter 7

Passport Information: U.S. Government
http://www.unitedstates.org/passport.php?source=google
http://travel.state.gov/passport/passport_1738.html

Service for Passport and Visa:
http://www.travisa.com/passporc.htm
http://www.passportsandvisas.com/index.asp

Currency conversion:
http://www.gocurrency.com/
http://www.xe.com/
http://www.x-rates.com/(nice tables)

Airport Terminal maps
http://www.gofox.com/flights/airportmaps.php http://www.
  skyteam.com/EN/travelResources/airportMgrSearch/index.jsp

More **International** Terminals:
http://www.worldairportguide.com/airport/airports.ehtml
Over 5000 U.S. Airports
http://find.mapmuse.com/interest/airports
Another good U.S. Airport terminal site:
http://www.airports.com/
Friendly Mapquest site:
http://www.mapquest.com/features/main.adp?page=airportmaps

Luggage/shrink wrapping
http://www.pprune.org/passengers-slf-self-loadingfreight/354111-
  shrink-wrapping-luggage.html
and
http://www.worldbaggage.com.au/cgibin/gen.cgi?action=genpage
  &pageid=secure_wrap

Chapter 10

U.S. Embassies
http://usembassy.state.gov/

Seating
http://www.seatguru.com/airlines/Northwest_Airlines/
  Northwest_Airlines_Boeing_747-200_Z.php
http://www.airlinequality.com/Product/seats_americas.htm
  (For seat size)

Chapter 11

List of European Airlines
http://www.etn.nl/lcosteur.htm

Embassy Websites: http://usembassy.state.gov/

Phone Country Codes

Country	Codes	Country	Codes
Afghanistan	93	China	86
Albania	355	Columbia	57
Algeria	213	Congo	242
Andorra	376	Croatia	385
Anguilla	1264	Cuba	53
Antigua & Barbuda	1268	Cyprus (North)	90392
Argentina	54	Cyprus (South)	357
Armenia	374	Czech Republic	420
Austria	43	Denmark	45
Azerbaijan	994	Dominica	1767
Bahamas	1242	Dominican-Republic	1809
Bahrain	973	Egypt	20
Bangladesh	880	El-Salvador	503
Barbados	1246	Equatorial-Guinea	240
Belarus	375	Estonia	372
Belgium	32	Falkland Islands	500
Bermuda	1441	Faroe Islands	298
Bosnia Herzegovina	387	Fiji	679
Botswana	267	Finland	358
Brazil	55	France	33
Brunei	673	Georgia	995
Bulgaria	359	Germany	49
Burundi	257	Gibraltar	350
Cambodia	855	Greece	30
Cameroon	237	Greenland	299
Canada	1	Grenada	1473
Cape Verde	238	Guadeloupe	590
Cayman Islands	1345	Guam	1671
Chile	56	Haiti	509

Country	Codes	Country	Codes
Hong Kong	852	Maldives	960
Hungary	36	Malta	356
Iceland	354	Mauritius	230
India	91	Mexico	52
Indonesia	62	Moldova	373
Iran	98	Monaco	377
Iraq	964	Mongolia	976
Ireland	353	Montserrat	1664
Israel	972	Morocco	212
Italy	39	Mozambique	258
Ivory Coast	225	Myanmar (Burma)	95
Jamaica	1876	Namibia	264
Japan	81	Nepal	977
Jordan	962	Netherlands	31
Kazakhstan	7	New Zealand	64
Kenya	254	Nigeria	234
Korea (North)	850	Paraguay	595
Korea (South)	82	Peru	51
Kuwait	965	Philippines	63
Kyrgyz Republic	996	Poland	48
Latvia	371	Portugal	351
Lebanon	961	Puerto Rico	1787
Lesotho	266	Qatar	974
Libya	218	Reunion	262
Liechtenstein	423	Romania	40
Lithuania	370	Russia	7
Luxembourg	352	Rwanda	250
Macau	853	San Marino	378
Macedonia	389	Saudi Arabia	966
Madagascar	261	Senegal	221
Malawi	265	Serbia & Montenegro	381
Malaysia	60	Seychelles	248

Country	Codes	Country	Codes
Singapore	65	Tonga	676
Slovakia	421	Trinidad & Tobago	1868
Slovenia	386	Tunisia	216
South Africa	27	Turkey	90
Spain	34	Turkmenistan	993
Sri Lanka	94	Turks & Caicos Islands	1649
St.Kitts & Nevis	1869	Uganda	256
St.Lucia	1758	Ukraine	380
St.Vincent & Grenadines	1784	United Arab Emirates	971
Sudan	249	United Kingdom	44
Suriname	597	USA	1
Swaziland	268	Uzbekistan	998
Sweden	46	Venezuela	582
Switzerland	41	Vietnam	84
Syria	963	Virgin Islands (British)	1284
Taiwan	886	Virgin Islands (US)	1340
Tanzania	255	Yemen	967
Thailand	66	Zambia	260
Togo	228	Zimbabwe	263

Voltage Regulator/Plug adapter chart

Following is an up-to-date guide, as of January, 2007 on voltage in foreign countries. In general, all references to 110 Volt apply to the range from 110 Volt to 160 Volt. Reference to 220 Volt is to the range from 220 Volt to 260 Volt. Voltage varies within country, depending on locations. Pictured below are the plug adapters that fit the country associated with the "letter".

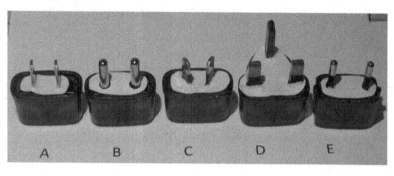

Afghanistan	220	E
Albania	220	B
Algeria	127/220	B,E
American Samoa	120/220	A,B,C
Angola	220	B
Anguila	240	D
Antigua/Barbuda	230	A,D
Argentina	220	B,C
Armenia	220	B
Aruba	115	A,B
Australia	240	C
Austria	230	B
Azerbajian	220	B
Azores	220	B,E

Bahamas	120	A
Bahrain	220	D,E
Bali	220	B
Bangladesh	220	B,E
Barbados	115	A
Belarus	220	B
Belgium	230	B
Belize	110	A
Benin	220	E
Bermuda	120	A
Bhutan	220	B,D
Bolivia	110/220	A,B
Bosnia-Herzegovina	220	B
Botswana	220	D, E
Brazil	110/220	A, B
Bulgaria	220	B
Burkina	220	B
Burma (Myanmar)	230	D, E
Burundi	220	B
Cambodia	120/220	A, B
Cameroon	220	B
Canada	120	A
Canary Islands	220	B
Cape Verde Islands	220	B
Cayman Islands	120	A
Central African Republic	220	B
Chad	220	B, E
Chile	220	B
China	220	B, C
Colombia	110	A
Comoros	220	B

Congo	220	B
Costa Rica	120	A
Croatia	220	B
Cuba	120	A
Curacao	110/220	A, B
Cyprus	240	B, D
Czech Republic	220	B
Denmark	230	B
Djibouti	220	B
Dominica	230	B, D
Dominican Republic	110	A
Ecuador	120	A
Egypt	220	B
El Salvador	115	A
England	240	D
Eritrea	220	B, E
Estonia	220	B
Ethiopia	220	B, E
Fiji	240	C
Finland	230	B
France	230	B
Gabon	220	B
Gambia	220	D
Georgia	220	B
Germany	230	B
Ghana	220	B, D, E
Greece	230	B
Greenland	220	B
Grenada	230	B, D, E
Grenadines	230	B, D, E
Guadeloupe	220	B

Guam	120	A
Guatemala	120	A
Guinea	220	B
Guyana	110	A
Haiti	110	A
Honduras	110	A
Hong Kong	220	D, E
Hungary	220	B
Iceland	220	B
India	220	B, E
Indonesia	220	B
Iran	220	B
Iraq	220	B, D, E
Ireland	220	D
Israel	230	B
Italy	230	H
Ivory Coast	220	B
Jamaica	110	A
Japan	100	A
Jordan	220	B, D
Kazakhstan	220	B
Kenya	240	B, D, E
Kirghizia	220	B
Korea	110/220	A, B
Kuwait	240	B, D, E
Laos	220	A, B
Latvia	220	B
Lebanon	220	B
Lesotho	240	B, E
Liberia	120	A, D
Libya	230	B, E

Liechtenstein	220	B
Lithuania	220	B
Luxembourg	230	B
Macao	220	B, E
Macedonia	220	B
Madagascar	220	B
Malawi	230	D
Malaysia	240	D
Mali	220	B
Malta	240	D
Martinique	220	B
Mauritania	220	B
Mauritius	230	B, D, E
Mexico	120	A
Moldova	220	B
Monaco	220	B
Mongolia	220	B
Morocco	220	B, E
Mozambique	220	B
Myanmar (Burma)	230	D, E
Namibia	220	E
Nepal	220	B, E
Netherlands	230	B
New Zealand	230	C
Nicaragua	120	A
Niger	220	B
Nigeria	230	D, E
Norway	230	B
Oman	240	D, E
Pakistan	230	B, E
Panama	120	A

Papua New Guinea	240	C
Paraguay	220	B
Peru	110/220	A, B
Philippines	110/220	A, B
Poland	220	B
Portugal	230	B, E
Puerto Rico	120	A
Qatar	240	D, E
Romania	220	B
Russian Federation	220	B
Rwanda	220	B
St. Kitts-Nevis	230	D, E
St. Lucia	240	D
St. Vincent	230	D
Saudi Arabia	127/220	A, B, D
Scotland	220	D
Senegal	220	B
Seychelles	240	D, E
Sierra Leone	230	D, E
Singapore	230	B, D, E
Slovakia	220	B
Slovenia	220	B
Solomon Islands	220	C, D
Somalia	220	B
South Africa	230	F
Spain	230	B
Sri Lanka	230	E
Sudan	240	B, D
Surinam	110/220	A, B
Swaziland	230	E
Sweden	230	B

Switzerland	230	G
Syria	220	B
Tahiti	127/220	A, B
Taiwan	220	B, C
Tajikistan	220	B
Tanzania	230	D, E
Thailand	220	A, B
Tonga	110/220	A, C
Trinidad & Tobago	115/230	A, D
Tunisia	220	B
Turkey	220	B
Turkmenistan	220	B
Uganda	240	D, E
Ukraine	220	B
United Arab Emirates	220	D, E
United Kingdom	240	D
United States	120	A
Uruguay	220	B
Uzbekistan	220	B
Venezuela	120	A
Vietnam	120/220	A, B
Virgin Islands	120	A
Wales	220	D, E
Western Samoa	230	C
Yemen	220	B, D, E
Yugoslavia	220	B
Zaire	220	B, E
Zambia	220	B, D
Zimbabwe	220	D, E

Airplane Seating, Interior

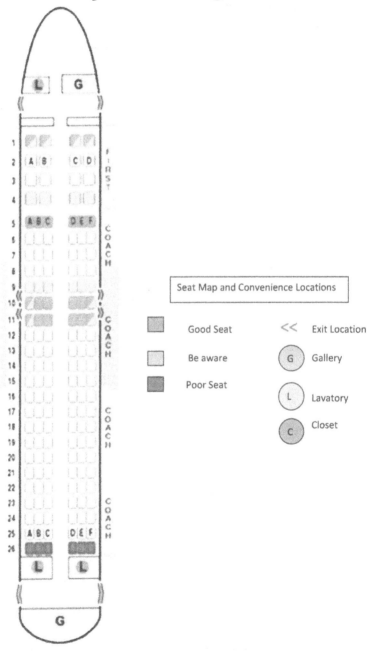

Seat Map and Convenience Locations

	Good Seat	<<	Exit Location
	Be aware	G	Gallery
	Poor Seat	L	Lavatory
		C	Closet

WORLD TIME ZONES

From: http://www.worldtimezone.com/

Below map provided with permission: Gheos.com

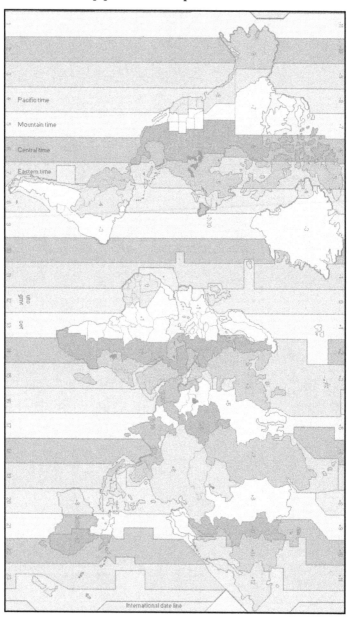

FREE BONUS!!

Please take advantage of the Bonus Materials! Visit my website:

www.SecretsForTravelSurvival.com

www.EugeneREhmann.com

Epilogue

Author and his wife, Maryann

I've been asked by a number of people about some of my personal preferences regarding travel itself. Realizing we're all different, and that some of us are a bit odd, I will share what I like:

Flying

1) I prefer *not* traveling either leg on the weekend. Mostly, flights are more available during the week, except for some commuter legs.

2) If I have a long flight (like over five hours), I don't mind taking a red-eye— an overnight flight. I can sleep reasonably well, particularly if I remember a few of those conveniences mentioned in Chapter 9. And if I'm

leaving from a city in which I've worked, or in which I enjoy touring, I have that whole last day to enjoy the city. Usually, an overnight flight gets me home sometime mid-morning, so I can conduct business that same day.

3) I like to travel as light as possible as far as clothing. I *always* take more than I need, thinking that I "need" more shirts, etc. Listen: washing out clothes by hand doesn't mean the end of life as we know it. A small container of liquid detergent (just a few ounces) makes that possible. Most clothes dry overnight; most hotels have irons, if not in the room, then with room service. Regarding more formal clothes like suits, etc., almost all hotels have one-day service. If I can only check one bag, so much the better. With the airlines beginning to charge for *every* bag checked, it is more and more tempting to have your carry-on bag be your primary bag. The computer and work briefcase can go under your seat.

4) As for reservations, I use any and all services, including a travel agent from time to time. Sometimes good travel agents can find or make those connections that don't seem possible through online sources, once again proving that there is still a place for humans. For instance, most online reservation sites don't "think" very well. If a particular flight is too expensive or booked up, maybe going through another city is the way. For example, I need to get to Buenos Aires; all flights seem booked that get me in from the United States. I can perhaps get in to make a scheduled meeting, if I go through Montevideo, Uruguay, or even Santiago, Chile (across the Andes!), just as cheaply, or close. Also, because of big time-zone differences, it might be useful to fly in to a nearby city,

spend the night, and fly into your destination city early the next morning. The same reasoning is also true for U.S. cities. There are many, many U.S. cities that have no direct flight from your hometown. Carefully consider getting to that destination city by one-stopping to or through a city you may not think about readily.

5) Negotiate, negotiate, negotiate! This, of course, works best when dealing directly with humans. Ask about discounts: senior, corporate, special offers. If you have a budget that you really don't want to exceed or can't, deal with a travel agent if your finances are close to "market price." Tell him you want and need to go but can't spend more than a certain amount. Ask him to call you when he finds a plan that meets your need. It's surprising how much can be done! That's also true with getting specific, hard-to-obtain arrival times.

Accommodations

1) I don't have to stay in a four- or five-star hotel. I'd rather stay in a borderline questionable area in or close to the center of town, for the sake of being close to the history of the town and close to old establishments, than be housed in a nicer hotel. It's a gross generalization, but most cities used to be vibrant in their downtowns and many have declined in the last several decades, businesses finding less expensive, perhaps "less dangerous" environs outside of the downtown. By the same token, many museums and many of the finer restaurants are located in the downtown or central part of the city. I like to be able to walk to those.

2) I've come to want wireless Internet, but otherwise I like hotels to be clean, quiet, and well located—in that order.

3) I don't mind buying from a local grocery store and eating some snacks or meals in my room. Find the local store, and go shop! (The local restaurant is buying the food they prepare for you at a local grocery store.)

Local Travel

1) Cabs are usually very reasonable.
2) Don't hesitate to inquire about a driver, for several hours or for a day. Again, they can often be very, very reasonable, often good guides, and quite convenient.

Economics/Spending

Learn enough in your preparation study to have a good sense about the local economy. The tendency is very, very clearly for foreign countries to charge tourists (especially American tourists) American prices. We often assume that a meal in a foreign country will be about the same cost as in America. Or we think that shopping will be about the same cost. Mostly this is not so. In spite of the ups and downs of the value of the U.S. dollar, we still have one of the best and highest standards of living in the world.

When in a foreign country, using good thinking, consider the standard of living of the average person there. Where do *they* eat? Where do *they* shop? If you suspect that the hotel concierge is in some unholy alliance with local business sharks, all of whom want to get all of your money, then ask the bellboy or ask a local merchant. Some of the personnel at an American embassy can be most helpful. I've never been steered down that long, dark alley that we all imagine in the back of our minds. Again, use common sense.

BUY A SHARE OF THE FUTURE IN YOUR COMMUNITY

These certificates make great holiday, graduation and birthday gifts that can be personalized with the recipient's name. The cost of one S.H.A.R.E. or one square foot is $54.17. The personalized certificate is suitable for framing and will state the number of shares purchased and the amount of each share, as well as the recipient's name. The home that you participate in "building" will last for many years and will continue to grow in value.

Here is a sample SHARE certificate:

YES, I WOULD LIKE TO HELP!

I support the work that Habitat for Humanity does and I want to be part of the excitement! As a donor, I will receive periodic updates on your construction activities but, more importantly, I know my gift will help a family in our community realize the dream of homeownership. **I would like to SHARE in your efforts against substandard housing in my community!** *(Please print below)*

PLEASE SEND ME _____ SHARES at $54.17 EACH = $ $_____

In Honor Of: _____

Occasion: (Circle One)   HOLIDAY   BIRTHDAY   ANNIVERSARY

       OTHER: _____

Address of Recipient: _____

Gift From: _____ *Donor Address:* _____

Donor Email: _____

I AM ENCLOSING A CHECK FOR $ $_____ PAYABLE TO HABITAT FOR HUMANITY <u>OR</u> PLEASE CHARGE MY VISA OR MASTERCARD *(CIRCLE ONE)*

Card Number _____ Expiration Date: _____

Name as it appears on Credit Card _____ Charge Amount $ _____

Signature _____

Billing Address _____

Telephone # Day _____ Eve _____

PLEASE NOTE: Your contribution is tax-deductible to the fullest extent allowed by law.
Habitat for Humanity • P.O. Box 1443 • Newport News, VA 23601 • 757-596-5553
www.HelpHabitatforHumanity.org